Scriptures for the

$\mathcal{L}$ent 2008
Behold the Lamb of God

Simon Peter Iredale

A Lenten Study Based on the Revised Common Lectionary

 Abingdon Press

A Lenten Study Based on the Revised Common Lectionary

BEHOLD THE LAMB OF GOD

Copyright © 2007 by Abingdon Press

Scripture quotations in this publication, unless otherwise indicated, are from the New Revised Standard Version of the Bible, copyright 1989, Division of Christian Education of the National Council of the Churches of Christ in the United States of America. Used by permission. All rights reserved.

All readings taken from the Revised Common Lectionary © 1992 Consultation on Common Texts are used by permission.

ISBN-13: 978-0-687-49235-0

Manufactured in the United States of America

07 08 09 10 11 12 13 14 15 16—10 9 8 7 6 5 4 3 2 1

Contents

Introduction

To be asked to accompany Christian people through their Lent and Easter studies is as much a source of apprehension as it is an honor. While there are many other important moments in the church year, Easter is like ascending the Himalayas rather than going for a pleasant walk in the park. For this reason, every Christian takes the days of preparation through Lent with utmost seriousness. As we pass through the Sundays of Lent, we will explore together the foundations of our common faith, testing ourselves through reflection and prayer to see how strong these foundations are in our hearts.

In our journey together, we will visit the first garden of paradise and seek to understand how the events that Genesis describes touched every succeeding human generation. We shall consider the great risk of faith that we each take through the example of the patriarch Abraham, the father of faith, and, with the incredulous Nicodemus, be reminded of the way that every believer must be "born from above" in the Holy Spirit. We shall follow Paul in his loving struggle with the early church communities as he sought to explain to them the way Christ was the fulfillment of the Law and the life of every living creature under heaven.

Between these higher peaks, as we ascend, there is time to refresh our understanding of the virtues of patience, humility, and endurance—the things that are the marks of mature discipleship. Here we shall also reflect on how even though we live in the world we are not subject to its passing values and preoccupations. Before we reach the summit of Easter Sunday, we must pass through the valley of the shadow of death and another garden, Gethsemane, the garden of decision. There we will strive to understand what Christ has achieved for us through his suffering. On Easter Sunday, we will arrive at the third garden, that of the Resurrection.

As we journey together through these peaks, valleys, and gardens, my prayer is that God will have given you something special to mark this year's celebration—a new resolve, a sense of sins forgiven, or a deeper insight into the universe of compassion that God turns, like a loving face, toward our humanity.

Humanity's Problem, God's Solution

Scriptures for Lent:
The First Sunday
Genesis 2:15-17; 3:1-7
Romans 5:12-19
Matthew 4:1-11

We recently acquired a black cat that is about a year old. Before we brought her home from the cat shelter, she had lived in a cage. After we had given her the chance to get used to the house and the family, the great day came when she could get out into the back yard. Our yard is not exactly the garden of Eden; but to a young cat with no experience of all those wonderful things that hop and flutter by, it must have seemed pretty close to it. I remember watching her explore one day. Suddenly her eyes picked up the flight of a large bumblebee. Before I could shout a warning, she was after the bee, leaping deer-like into the air and finally holding the bee down between her paws. At this point I sprinted down the garden calling her name—but too late. The bee, without any choice left and no doubt convinced in its little buzzing head that its time was up, stung her. Our cat disappeared in a blur and spent the next hour in agony, licking the sore place.

Why am I telling you this? On reflection, it seems to me that this simple experience explains something about the first reading for this Sunday, Genesis 2:15-17; 3:1-7. Human beings are set down in a wonderful place filled with all sorts of possibilities for fun and creativity. However, for reasons that ultimately escape us, there has to be an element of risk in all this—that we have the freedom to ignore God's warnings to us (as the cat ignored me!) and that there are some things that, treated the wrong way, can do us harm. Despite all the fondness I have for the cat and despite knowing what was likely to happen, she still received her sting. Well, humanity, in the persons of Adam and Eve, certainly received their "sting"; and we are still living with the consequences. We will look at that story again together.

The second reading, Romans 5:12-19, explores the idea of the gift of new life and justification in

Paul's understanding of the old Adam and the new Adam, Jesus Christ. In the Gospel reading, Matthew 4:1-11, we enter into Christ's temptation in an attempt to understand and appreciate how through his suffering love Jesus Christ has brought us back into the first garden of God's presence.

THE HEAVENLY GARDEN
GENESIS 2:15-17; 3:1-7

When we open the pages of the Book of Genesis, the "Book of Beginnings," we stretch back to the first moments of our relationship to God as human beings. It is like sitting in front of a symphony orchestra. The bows are poised, the brass players and woodwinds raise their instruments, the conductor makes a brief gesture of attention, and the first few notes swell into a wonderful first theme. The music of Genesis, sometimes plaintive and tragic, at other times full of hope and joy, weaves through the whole Bible, finding its greatest and most cosmos-filling climax in the accounts of the Resurrection. Genesis has profound things to say to our situation in ways that no other field of human knowledge can hope to emulate. This is why the Genesis stories continue to be an inspiration to artists, musicians, and writers. Over the millennia it speaks persuasively to our deepest experience of being human.

Adam and Eve were in the garden because they belonged there. It was their first home. As the keepers and tenders of the garden, they shared in the creativity of God. They could wonder at the beauty of what God had made and walk with God in the cool of the day (Genesis 3:8). Only one tree was forbidden to the heavenly couple (2:16-17). Remember my cat? If I could have communicated with her adequately, I would have said, "Chase anything you like, but keep away from the bees!" God set a limit here that proceeded solely from love. What appeared to be inviting and "a delight to the eyes" (3:6) held within it a whole world of suffering.

"Why is that tree there in the first place?" we might be tempted to ask. "If God loves us that much, why not take the cause of our fall completely away?" Here we enter into a mystery that exceeds what we are able to understand. What we can say is that God wills for us to respond freely with love rather than to be puppets without choice. The possibility of the Fall has to exist. Respecting our freedom, God risks all and gives a solemn warning: "You shall die." Adam and Eve did not heed God's warning.

Have you ever heard the expression "Be careful what you ask for, you might get it?" Sometimes we ask God for something repeatedly because we are so sure that what we ask for is the answer to all our problems. All we need is the divine green light, and everything will be wonderful. Then later, by some means, we discover what a disaster it would have been if God had said yes. Having had this experience a few times, I tend to recommend the advice of the Egyptian desert father who, in the fourth century, said that when we pray we should simply say to God, "As you know, as you will ... and in times of trouble, help me." We do not know what is good for us; and we, therefore, will often find ourselves asking for the wrong things. Surely, if we believe that God loves us, then we can also trust God to lead us in the ways that will be best for us.

This model of our way of praying is one way to understand the drama of the serpent, Eve, and Adam. However, we understand the difficult role of the serpent. We feel that the moment the serpent suggested that Adam and Eve were being offered something that would "do them good" or something that was being kept from them, the tragic conclusion seems inevitable. Eve believed eating the fruit would bring wisdom (3:6). Wisdom, in itself, is a genuinely good thing for which to seek. The serpent implied that God kept them from such wisdom on purpose. "God knows that when you eat of it your eyes will be opened, and you will be like God, knowing good and evil" (verse 5). The result was a fall into a world where evil became for them a real possibility; and perfect good, though longed for, seemed to be forever just out of reach. Their nakedness was spiritual as well as physical.

The creation of Adam and Eve and their garden home offers a picture of God's intent for all creation. Think of that. Each of us has been created to walk with God in the cool of the day. Similarly, we share their fall and their exile from the heavenly garden. By God's grace, however, we can still appreciate the beauty of a sunset. In this way, we can experience little reminders of God's presence when we are willing to see them. If we marvel at God's world today, what must it have been like before sin cast its shadow?

What insights do you gain from the fall of Adam and Eve about your life in God's world? What do these Scripture passages say to you about God? about human beings?

THE FIRST AND SECOND ADVENT
ROMANS 5:12-19

When I was at the university as a young man, I remember a Christian saying to me, "If God seems far away, who has moved?" At the time it seemed an odd thing to say, but I now realize he was speaking about the subject Paul addressed in this second reading. We find Paul in the middle of a difficult argument, packed with new ideas for his listeners. His audience was probably made up of Jews who already had allegiance to Christ but were confused about what their attitude should be to Jesus

Christ on the one hand and to the Law received by Moses on the other. Paul addressed this confusion more directly in Romans 9. For those to whom Paul wrote, this was not just a matter of the content of the Law; it was a matter of national religious identity.

For the Jews of the first century, and of today, the covenant with God and the laws received by Moses were what defined them as a people. They saw themselves, with good reason, as different from the nations around them. The Law, taken together with the continuous offerings at the Temple in Jerusalem, constituted what it was to be the people of Israel. So it is understandable that if they thought Paul was suggesting that the Law, with the advent of Christ, was now somehow of less importance, it would cause them a great deal of worry. Just what were they getting themselves into if Christian faith meant abandoning everything that made sense of their lives?

One way of understanding the Ten Commandments is that they are a blueprint for human society. Every commandment refers to an aspect of human relationship with God and with the community. Every commandment, if kept, means that human beings have a chance of living together in peace. Obeying God's law gives a family resemblance to God even with the effects of the Fall.

To take a modern example, think of the laws that govern a game of football. The players might be willing to play the game; but if there are no rules about how many can play on each side, how many balls are on the field at any one time, or who decides split decisions, the result is chaos. The players need the rules because without them they would not be capable of agreeing on whether a team had won or not. Paul said that after the fall of humanity, the effects of sin meant that chaos took over. We had lost the capability of knowing what was right. When he said that "death exercised dominion from Adam to Moses," he vividly expressed the reality of what it is to fall away from God—spiritual and physical death (verse 14). This is just common sense since God is the very source of life. God is the One who is. Apart from God, we cannot exist.

So, to return to our football image, the players for this enormous length of time became less and less certain of how to play the game, since no one was there to say, "This is how you play it." Humanity was in a pitiable state. God's supreme creation appeared to be heading relentlessly toward nothingness. The laws given to Moses and all the events of the sacred history—the Exodus and the coming into the Promised Land—were given to humanity like a hand offered to someone who is just about to fall over a cliff. They were given by God as an act of supreme love and compassion.

Humanity, in the covenant people of Israel, took God's outstretched hand.

Paul's listeners would have understood completely. This is what they had learned at their parents' knees.

Now Paul takes them further. The Law is not the end but the beginning of God's answer to humanity's tragic predicament. While trying to keep the Law will indeed give humanity some idea of who God is and what glory they have fallen away from, our poor efforts quite simply will never be able to bring us back into the heavenly garden. Before Christ, the Law did its holy work of "bringing us into remission"—but the Law could not cure us since we could not keep it perfectly.

Suddenly, through Paul's insights, we become aware, like the sun coming out from behind a cloud, of just how much God loves us. In Christ, as the Second Adam, Paul traced the illness back to its root in the garden of Eden. Christ heals the illness with his own abundant life. Adam tragically brought a downward spiral into death; Jesus Christ as Second Adam, however, brings justification and life (verse 18). In spiritual terms, when we accept Christ, we re-enter the heavenly garden; and Adam's first ancient trespass is cancelled.

In verses 15-17, Paul expresses God's work in Jesus Christ as a gift. What is the nature of a gift? It is not something earned or expected. You would feel rightly annoyed if your employer gave you your wages as a gift instead of as just compensation for the hard work you have put in. Similarly, if on your birthday you only received presents that you had already ordered online and have passed to your family to "give" to you, they would seem rather hollow gifts.

A gift is always motivated by love in order to be a gift. That cuts out things such as bribes or gifts that bite you since these would not be motivated by love but by self-interest or actually designed to do you harm. If you recall, we were thinking about what we ask God for in prayer. Being love itself, God wants to give us loving gifts; but we still insist on asking for "a serpent instead of a fish" (Matthew 7:10).

The only thing you can do with a true gift lovingly given is to accept it. This is what God offers us in Christ. We have not earned or deserved what Christ has done for us. That would be not only beyond our individual powers but beyond the powers of all humanity. God's motivation, if I can dare use such a word, is a love that goes infinitely beyond our human understanding of what love means. There really are no strings attached. We are simply asked to turn toward God and accept the gift of Christ. We are so used to imperfect human arrangements having terms and conditions that I often think we struggle to understand, even as Christians, that God offers us a free gift. Perhaps that is part of the process of convalescence, too. As we receive that gift, which is God's very nature through the Holy Spirit, we will find all kinds of ways to thank God. The gift is not an end but the beginning. Paul set the Law in the context of this loving gift. The Christians of Rome understood that Christ fulfils and confirms the Law. Christ invites all to enter an utterly new age of life with God. "Thanks be to God for his inexpressible gift!" (2 Corinthians 9:15).

How do you understand the idea of a gift? In what ways does Paul's image of God's justification and life through Jesus Christ as a gift inform your relationship with God?

THE PERFECT HUMAN BEING
MATTHEW 4:1-11

Strangely, the Gospel reading brings us back full circle to Genesis. Once again "Adam," in the person of Jesus, is placed in a situation where the human being's resolve is tested. This time it is not a lush garden but a desert, and the tempter is clearly the devil. We seem to have travelled a long way from the first reading; and indeed, in terms of time, from the first Adam to Christ is a period of time that is difficult to imagine. I think, however, that we can begin to understand why the Holy Spirit led Jesus out into the desert before he began his ministry. If everything we hope for from the Son of God (who is also the Son of Man) can

come to pass, we need to understand how Jesus was exposed to the most the tempter could throw at him and how he overcame those insidious suggestions.

Earlier in my life I lived in Egypt, where I taught English. I frequently had the opportunity to go out into the desert since I was interested in the history of the early monastic movement represented by the writings of the desert saints. Often, the only way to reach these remote monasteries was to catch a taxi along the road from Cairo to Alexandria, follow the journey on a map, and at what looked like an appropriate place simply get out and walk. Usually there was a little village not far from the road where someone would point you up a rough track that led through stony hills into the desert.

In the fourth century, this desert was filled with monks and hermits living as solitaries or in community. They had left the "fleshpots" of Alexandria, following the great example of Saint Antony of Egypt and others with romantic names, such as Moses the Black, to lead lives of utter simplicity and devoted to prayer. The desert, for them, was the spiritual front line. They left the cities partly to escape from distraction but mainly to imitate Christ in his wilderness wanderings.

The desert is a special place. As I plodded along in search of my monastery, I was immediately aware of the extremes of the place:

the heat, the lack of shade, and the isolation. What was also striking was the tremendous silence. Our lives, especially in the 21st century, are so noisy that we are rarely free from some kind of background sound, whether welcome or unwelcome. In the desert, the most you can hear is the scuttle of sand grains as the wind snatches them up and dashes them around the dunes. The waves of heat give things in the distance an air of unreality. When I came in sight of the massive walls of the monastery approached through a scant plantation of palms, it was as if the palm trees were dancing together, rising on streams of hot air. Far in the distance the monks saw me; and, the huge doors opening, one of them in his traditional black habit stood motionlessly waiting for me to arrive. He must have stood there for ten minutes without stirring. Then, when I came up to him, he offered me the traditional gifts of hospitality: bread and salt.

The image that I find the most useful when thinking about Jesus in the desert is of an athlete in training. It is ironic that people with little religious belief will still often take on strict regimes of training and fasting (in the sense of strict dietary rules) in pursuit of the body beautiful and a few more seconds shaved off their performance on the track. Their asceticism and determination rivals that of the monks. If people could put the same kind of self-sacrifice and

dedication into their spiritual lives, the world would become a little more as God intends it to be.

Jesus stripped himself in the silence of the desert of all the things that might have offered him support or distract him from the great task that lay ahead— family, friends, even the rites of religion that had been familiar to him since childhood. In that isolation, the voice of the tempter came to him. There is much to say about the nature of the temptations offered to Christ. In fact, we can never exhaust their meaning. Have you ever wondered how we actually know about them? One can only suggest that Jesus, sitting with his disciples, perhaps in one of those frequent retreats into the desert with which he punctuated his ministry, told them of his experiences.

What would it be like to fill every human need, to abolish hunger, to satisfy every human appetite so that no one ever again suffered through the inequalities of the world's economy. Surely that would be something worth having. After all, a great many of humanity's wars have been fought over scarce resources. How much grief you could bring to an end. This is the character of the first temptation: turning stones into bread. Nevertheless, Jesus resisted the tempter's suggestion. When we think about it, those inequalities, the fact that children in one country go hungry while others on the other side of the world are fed, is also an aspect of the fall. We would have enough to go around if we were not so fatally divided by pride and hostility, greed and the desire for power. Jesus came to strike at the root of sin from which all these inequalities spring. To accept this temptation would make Jesus the ruler of the world but not the savior of our souls. This temptation is too little to ask of him.

Our popular imagination is full of super heroes. One can scarcely go to the movies today without being presented with a comic-book character brought to life with full special effects. It says something odd about how we understand heroism—that you somehow have to be more than human to be heroic.

The ancient world also had its fair share of heroes and heroines. Homer's poems describe titanic battles between the Greeks and the Trojans. The Greek and Roman gods also had their human heroes, such as Hercules, whose superhuman feats earned them a place in the stars. Even the achievements of historical figures such as Alexander and Caesar were awe-inspiring enough to give them the status of super heroes in the eyes of their contemporaries. They believed such leaders proved their divine credentials by main force.

How easy it would have appeared to be for Jesus to don this shining robe of invincibility. How easy to right all the wrongs of his time, to drive the Romans out of Israel, to convince the people of

his divinity by spectacular signs. To accept this temptation would leave humanity as slaves because we would not be free to choose. Who could genuinely follow a Jesus who leaped tall buildings with a single bound? Such dramatic signs would deprive us of choice. Many people who heard Jesus stayed and became disciples, and many more turned away. They had a choice. This temptation, too, is too little to ask of him.

Frustrated so far, the tempter threw everything he thought he had into the ring. It is interesting here, if you compare the accounts in Luke's Gospel with this one in Matthew, that Satan said to Jesus, "To you I will give their glory and all this authority; for it has been given over to me, and I give it to anyone I please" (Luke 4:6). There is something about the corrupting power of wealth that makes one wonder whether the devil is not actually lying at this point. If nothing in the whole world can touch Jesus' intention to deliver all creation from captivity, then the tawdry pleasures of wealth and human power will scarcely tempt him. Yet, again, this temptation is too little to ask of Jesus.

Jesus emerged from these temptations as the perfect human being, perfect in the sense that after Adam and Eve, only Jesus has lived the life for which human beings were created. Every man and woman can see in Christ's perfect humanity, glorified in the Resurrection, not only God's solution to humanity's problem but the wonder of every faithful person's destiny: fellowship with God for ever.

How do the temptations in the wilderness speak to you about contemporary Christian life? How do Jesus' responses to the temptations offer you guidance in your Christian journey?

The Risk of Faith

Scriptures for Lent:
The Second Sunday
Genesis 12:1-4a
Romans 4:1-5, 13-17
John 3:1-17

Sea swimming in the British Isles is always a challenge. Of course, there are plenty of opportunities to visit swimming pools where one can luxuriate in specially heated water; but it just is not the same thing as the cry of the gulls and the tang of the salt. Given that you have reasonably good weather, the beach will offer at least the appearance of warmth; but experienced swimmers know better. They know how cold the sea is at any time of year. It is quite amusing watching the way people enter the sea. Some will procrastinate for ages, sidling up to the water's edge, wetting their toes, trying to nerve themselves to go further. Others will undergo the torment of going in a bit at a time. The more resolute dive straight in and are soon telling others how wonderful the water is.

The step of faith is quite similar to this. One can spend years procrastinating. People will find all sorts of apparently good reasons not to take that step. Faith always requires a moment of risk. We move from warm, dry land to the unknown embrace of the sea. What is it going to be like? One thing is for certain; we shall only know by doing it.

Today's readings circle around this decision to trust God and take the step of faith. We begin with the call to Abraham (called Abram at this stage in his relationship with God) in Genesis 12:1-4a. In Romans 4:1-5, 13-17, we explore Paul's profound understanding of Abraham's significance. Finally, with the wonderful story of Jesus and Nicodemus in John 3:1-17, we think about the characteristics of a person who has taken the step of faith, who has been "born from above," who lives the life of the Spirit.

THE BLESSING
OF THE FAITHFUL
GENESIS 12:1-4a

What are the things that make us feel good about ourselves? Going from the least important to the most important, I suppose you could start with something as simple as habits and routines. In my military experience of being on deployment in the Middle East where your usual routines have been completely swept away, it was interesting to see what people did to help them feel at least a little at home in a completely new, and perhaps hostile, environment. Some people brought their music, a photo album, or one of their hobbies. What mattered to me most was having a decent cup of tea in the morning. You can tell I am a true Englishman! Even though I was staying in a tumbledown barracks in the middle of the desert, I made sure I had a cup of tea out of a china cup every morning before I went about my duties. In this simple way I coped with some of the strangeness of being away.

More important than mere routines and habits are our friends and families, the people who value us. In many ways, we understand ourselves in the context of these friendships and familial relationships. Human beings are sociable creatures. There is a limit to how much you can learn about yourself on your own. When you come into contact with others, it is as if a light shines on parts of your character that ordinarily would not be illuminated. For this reason, I believe, Christians are drawn into community with other Christians. We are meant to be parts of one body just by virtue of the way God

has made us. God teaches some things to us alone, but a great deal is taught through relationships with all their struggles and joys. Perhaps the most important source of our sense of our own value comes from those who love us and those whom we love.

I have invited you to reflect on all this so that we might have a better idea of just how much God asked Abraham to do. He was told to leave every single one of these things that not only gave him a sense of security but also everything that defined him as a person. In these ancient times, family—who your father and mother were and which tribe of people you belonged to—was the most important answer to the question, "Who am I?" Many parts of the world are still like this. If you ask someone from these countries who they are, they reply by telling you their family, tribe, or nation. If someone asked us in the West who we are, we may simply give our first name and not think to talk about our families until we get to know the other person a little bit better. Thus we are saying, "I am an individual" not "I belong to my family." I suppose this comes from our social history where the importance of the individual in commerce, education, and industry has been emphasized.

Another characteristic of the past is that ancient families were also connected to place. Where they lived defined them. We are still aware of the vestiges of this way of life in Britain. There are farming families that have looked after the same area of land, father to son, since the Middle Ages. The people living close to the land also seem to have long memories. I remember when I looked after some parishes in East Yorkshire. I was trying to get two villages to work more closely together, but they did not appear too keen on the idea. Finally, when I pushed the argument, they reluctantly muttered that they did not have much to do with the other village since they had supported the Parliamentarians during the Civil War! Most of us, however, are part of the constant ebb and flow of moving, following work and opportunities, which gradually detaches us from a sense of place. Abraham leaving his family land would have appeared as crazy a thing as wishing to start farming on the moon. Yet Abraham consciously broke these ties. He set off from Haran into the unknown, no doubt aware that he would never return.

Many people who have followed Abraham in this walk of faith in our own times have made the same kinds of sacrifices. In some cases, becoming Christian has meant being cast out by family and shunned by former friends. Christian faith is still actively persecuted in many parts of the world. It is humbling to think how much these people go through for Christ when our faith in the West attracts nothing more than indifference or gentle derision from time to time. I remember speaking to a Roman-ian Orthodox Christian who lived through the Soviet times. The Orthodox practice was to make the sign of the cross when they passed their church as a sign of their faith. This was forbidden. "What did you do?" I asked. "We made the sign of the cross with our tongues. The police didn't see, but God saw," was the answer.

In your story of faith there may have been hard and painful decisions or moments when you have had to leave something or someone important to you behind. For every Christian, Abraham is the father of faith and of the risk of trusting in God. We are blessed through him because he shows us what faith and trust in God look like.

When has your faith led to a "new land" or to leaving something behind? How was God with you during that time?

THE RIGHTEOUSNESS OF FAITH
ROMANS 4:1-5, 13-17

In order to explore Paul's argument in this passage, let us think again of Jesus' story of the prodigal son (Luke 15:11-32). Most of the time we tend to concentrate on the adventures (and misadventures) of the younger son. However, while all of this is going on, we are to assume the elder son is working diligently away, obeying his father's commands, and expecting to be given the rewards that his work and obedience deserve. That, of course, is the spark that ignites the complaint when the younger son came home and was given the gift of his father's love and was welcomed back into the family embrace. The elder son said, "What about me? Haven't I deserved better treatment? It's not fair!" There is much to say about the parable, but what is useful here is the contrast between something earned and something received as a gift. Remember that we looked at the characteristics of a gift in our last visit with Paul. This idea is crucial to how he understood our relationship to Christ.

Abraham becomes the person who first accepted God's gift for what it was. He believed the promise that God made to him despite the fact that it would take him far beyond the places and the people who gave him the greatest sense of his own security. There is nothing about the elder son of the parable in Abraham. He did not for a moment imagine that he had earned what God was doing for him. This simple faith and belief in the trustworthiness of God is what is counted as righteousness. I use the word *simple* here in the same way one says that a beam of light can be simple—it is not complicated by shadows or refracted in all sorts of directions. In point of fact, this simple faith of Abraham is the most difficult thing to achieve.

How many of us can say that we trust God with every aspect of our lives, hour by hour, day by day. We know that the Gospel teaches that kind of childlike simplicity. Jesus says in Matthew: "Truly I tell you, unless you change and become like children, you will never enter the kingdom of heaven" (Matthew 18:3). This reminds me of the day of my ordination. All kinds of important people (whether in their own opinion or in fact) turned up for the occasion. In my tradition, there is the requirement for a carefully orchestrated procession into church with all the dignitaries robed. Last, preceded by the church wardens carrying their wands of office, comes the bishop. As is always the danger with formal ceremony, the potential for disaster is high. As the procession wound into church, for some reason the bishop was delayed, so the church wardens were solemnly escorting no one at all. This was the moment when a four-year-old boy saw his chance. Wriggling out of his mother's arms, he fell in neatly behind the wardens, in the place of the bishop, and followed the procession up to the altar with a wide grin on his face. I was delighted. How appropriate it was that an innocent child should take the place of honor in Christ's church. I felt I had something to live up to in my ministry.

For those who have been Christian for many years, the elder son in us insists on getting involved, reminding us of how much we have done for the church, how often we have helped out on Sunday, and how many good and godly actions we have performed. These things, though not bad in themselves, fall short of the simple trust and belief of Abraham. We can so easily begin to think that we deserve something back from God for all the things we have done when it is always God who is the giver. We would be capable of nothing without God.

Paul had a particularly hard job on his hands since he was trying to change an entire point of view about how God should be worshiped. Many Jews of his time would have felt that if they lived in accordance with the laws of Moses, attended their synagogues, and performed all the external acts of piety, then God would treat them appropriately. While Paul, also a Jew, did not deride these examples of faithfulness, he emphasized Abraham's faith. He needed to get across to them the new freedom they had in Christ if they only would receive it. He did this by pointing to Abraham's faith. "Abraham believed God, and it was reckoned to him as righteousness" (Romans 4:3).

When have you struggled with the notion that you deserved something for your actions? What connections do you make between your faith and the idea of being rewarded for your actions?

WE SPEAK OF WHAT WE KNOW
JOHN 3:1-17

Sometimes I think we Christians tend to give the Pharisees a bad press. As with any large group of people, in their case it would be more helpful to think of them as a religious school. There are all kinds of different personalities involved. It is quite obvious that Jesus' ministry caused a great deal of questioning and inner conflict among the Pharisees. They genuinely did not know what to make of him. If we were living in their time, we would probably revere the Pharisees as godly and learned people who were examples to us of how to live according to God's covenant. Paul, as a young man growing up in Tarsus, sat at their feet and learned from them. This must have formed his thinking quite remarkably. Yet this is the same man who, after his experience of conversion on the Damascus road, became the Christian faith's greatest champion in the Roman world.

Nicodemus had a great deal to lose. He was, we are told, "a ruler of the Jews," which probably means he sat on the Jewish council, the Sanhedrin. Remember the nervous bathers approaching the sea? Here is someone who had spent a long time watching the sea from a distance, wondering what it was like to be in it. He felt strangely drawn to Jesus. He had heard, no doubt, what Jesus had said and done; but he still felt afraid of committing himself. Nicodemus's problem was, "How can I try swimming without getting wet?" The Scripture tells us that he "came to Jesus by night" (John 3:2).

What an extraordinary privilege actually to be in Jesus' presence to ask about faith. Imagine seeing him, as Nicodemus did, with your human eyes and being able to ask the questions that may be so often on your lips. I am sure every single person comes to faith in Christ in a different way. After all, if we believe that each human person is a unique creation, it is appropriate that each person's path to his or her Maker is similarly unique.

My entry into faith started with the Lord's Prayer. Rather like a doubting Nicodemus, I had watched Christian faith from afar I had even dared to dabble my toes in the waves by reading some of the classics of the Christian life, works by the saints and accounts of the early church. I was also attempting to swim without getting wet. It occurred to me one day that although I knew a great deal about faith, I had never prayed. This was my equivalent of jumping in at the deep end. In order to pray sincerely you have to admit the possibility that you are speaking to someone. I did not think, in my adult life, I had prayed in this way. So, not without an intense feeling of being foolish, I knelt and said the Lord's Prayer. That was the moment I left the safety of the shore and plunged into God's breakers. I am still "all at sea."

Nicodemus was not a ruler of the Jews for nothing. His opening words to Jesus sound like those of a politician, as though he was trying to smooth the way with Jesus, paying him the compliment of saying, "You must be someone special because of the things that you are able to do." Jesus, we remember from last Sunday's readings, had met this temptation before—that of the glory of the world that could be his—and promptly ignored the intended flattery. His first words to Nicodemus addressed with unerring accuracy the deep question that he had brought to Jesus for an answer. "No one can see the kingdom of God without being born from above" (verse 3).

Jesus' meetings with different people are well worth studying. No matter what else was going on, he seemed to be able to speak directly, almost intimately, to the person who spoke to him. He had so much time for each one, and his way with them was different on every occasion. With some, he could be devastatingly sharp, dropping them into the same trap they had tried to set for him. With others, he was serious and firm, pointing out the self-denial that the person—such as the rich young man (Matthew 19:16-22)—needed to have to enter the kingdom of heaven. With the poor and vulnerable, such as the Samaritan woman at the well (John 4:7-42), Jesus was gentle and did not judge. In every situation, while they were speaking to him, it was as if they were the only other person in the world; but his words touched the deepest causes of their sadness.

What Jesus said to Nicodemus left Nicodemus in an agony of confusion. How could he be asked to do something completely beyond his human powers? His mind raced to make sense of it, no doubt turning over various possibilities. This was just the problem; and it is often our problem, too.

In our human way, we need to see steps to solve a problem. We need to plan and develop strategies. If you imagine the arms of a cross, this is what one might call the "horizontal dimension" of the world. This is the dimension where we imagine we have power over what happens. There is also, however, the "vertical dimension" of the divine (and who knows how many other dimensions God wishes there to be), which, as where the bars of a cross intersect, cuts into our world with the suddenness of a miracle. We have no control over this dimension. We probably, in truth, have little control over the dimension of the world either; but we can receive what God gives us. This saying of Jesus for Nicodemus, and for us who read it, is straight from the vertical dimension of the divine. In human terms, no one can re-enter the womb; but in spiritual terms, without a spiritual re-birth, the life of a Christian does not begin to quicken at all.

Jesus used the example of the wind to help Nicodemus grasp the idea of being born of the Spirit. The Greek word translated as "wind" and as "Spirit" is pnuema, which also means "a current of air," "a breeze," or "the breath." The wind or Spirit of God can take many forms. Sometimes, the Spirit is the cool, refreshing Comforter who comes to our aid when our faith is hard-pressed. At other times, the Spirit needs to be like a strong wind that uproots and drives away the self-imposed barriers and restrictions we have created that prevent us from being alive.

The contrast between the mind-set of the world (the flesh) and that of faith (the Spirit) is something that can cause a great deal of concern, and occasionally sadness, in our relationships, particularly with those close to us. People of faith "march to a different drummer." As we follow Christ faithfully in our lives, we go through a process of profound change. We see things differently. We have different values and priorities. We are not so excited by the aims and goals that the rest of the world strains after. What we do in faith can seem to people of the world as irresponsible or just plain strange. This can sometimes make us feel the odd one out socially. In the world of the Spirit, to use a cooking image, oil and water do not mix. When you have given your life to Christ, you are indeed a "new creation" (2 Corinthians 5:17), which is a matter of great joy.

Poor Nicodemus did not get it. I imagine he was further confused when Jesus gave a prefiguring of the death he was to suffer (John 3:14). Like the bronze serpent lifted up by Moses in the wilderness (Numbers 21:9) to cure the people of Israel of their serpent bites, Christ would be lifted up on the cross to heal the ancient illness of sin. Until this great act of atonement had been achieved, it would not be possible for people such as Nicodemus to be born again. Yet, in his favor, he was at least curious enough to search after the answer to this spiritual problem that was bothering him. This conversation with Jesus obviously moved him closer to the kingdom of heaven since later in the Gospel of John we hear of him trying to defend Jesus when the Sanhedrin were determined to sentence Christ to death (John 7:50-51). He appears for a final time with the expensive herbs needed to preserve Jesus' broken body when he had been taken down from the cross (19:39).

If we, then, are people born of the Spirit, how are we to behave? The readings today have taught us that what we have received from God has been received as a loving gift. This gift, completely undeserved, is, however, a gift that introduces us into a completely new kind of life. Everything about us that belonged to the world will be gradually sifted away by the wind of the Spirit. Like Abraham, we shall be asked to make our own journey of faith, perhaps in a direction that will fill us equally with apprehension and excitement. While we are supposed to make human plans for our future, especially if we have others to care for, we must keep steadily before our minds and hearts our first allegiance to Christ. When he calls us to something utterly new and unexpected, we must be ready to respond. One thing is for certain; we shall not be allowed to stay safely within our comfort zone.

It may be that we, too, will have to spend time in the spiritual deserts of the world. As we lead this new life, people such as Nicodemus will come our way asking about what makes us different. We shall have to have an answer for them. We are a people who expect to see God working in the world around us, and we are willing to be co-workers with him. We have something in the military called a readiness state, which is how quickly you could be ready to go off on duty—as a chaplain in my case. The highest state of readiness is R1. I would like to think that our spiritual readiness state is also R1, that when God has something for us to do, or to learn, some area of service, then, like the wind, we can be off doing what God wills.

What does it mean to you to be born from above? to be born of the Spirit? What insights do these images of new birth offer for your life as a Christian?

The Faithful Life

Scriptures for Lent: The Third Sunday

Exodus 17:1-7
Romans 5:1-11
John 4:5-42

So far this Lent we have been thinking about the gift of Christ, that moment when we have understood that God is the source of life and that God offers life to all of us through Jesus Christ. We have thought about how much we sometimes need to leave behind when we take the first few steps of faith. Such steps often appear to us like a great risk because we may have to move away from the things that have previously given us comfort. Accepting Christ is an experience that changes us profoundly, and the way it happens is different for every person.

The Scriptures for the third Sunday of Lent show how God's gift works itself out in our lives. The same God who offers the gift of life through Jesus Christ supports us as we live our faith from day to day. The hymn "Father, Hear the Prayer We Offer" by L. M. Willis is a prayer for strength and courage in all circumstances of our Christian lives. The fourth stanza says, "Be our strength in hours of weakness / In our wanderings be our Guide." When we leave behind the green pastures for the often "steep and rugged pathway" of practical discipleship, we become like pilgrims who can only carry what is strictly necessary for our journey. What we carry is our faith in our life-giving God.

In Exodus 17:1-7, we join Moses and the people of the Exodus as they face their own temptation in the desert. Paul equips us with words of encouragement for the times of suffering and endurance in Romans 5:1-11. Finally, in John 4:5-42, which describes Jesus' meeting with the Samaritan woman at the well, we drink deeply from the source of our life, Christ the "spring of water gushing up to eternal life" (John 4:14).

IS THE LORD AMONG US OR NOT?
EXODUS 17:1-7

Perhaps you enjoyed watching the Olympic games on television as I did. Maybe you were fortunate enough to attend in person. I cannot claim to be an athletic person, but at least I recognize and admire the abilities of others. I am afraid I am a bit of an armchair athlete. Think of the sprinters, those young men and women who hurtle over the distance of 100 meters, every muscle straining to produce the last ounce of power. Their whole being is focused on just one thing: crossing the finish line before the other competitors. For them, in these few seconds, all the world retreats and nothing else matters. Such single-mindedness is admirable.

Paul spoke of such runners in the games in order to emphasize how one lives a faithful life in Christ. "Do you not know that in a race the runners all compete, but only one receives the prize? Run in such a way that you may win it. Athletes exercise self-control in all things; they do it to receive a perishable wreath, but we an imperishable one" (1 Corinthians 9:24-25). Paul may have been thinking of the sprinters, but my feeling is that the example he had in mind was that of the long-distance runners. These runners, in our own days as well, could not be more different from the sprinters who explode out of their blocks to run 100 meters. With the long-distance runners, everything unnecessary has been stripped away. With them, too, the world and all its preoccupations must retreat. Nothing matters but the next step, the next kilometer. They need to pace themselves in order to survive the grueling demands of the distance before them. While they are as focused as the sprinters, they have to have the mental toughness of setting intermediate targets—putting away from their minds how far they have left to cover. This is a far better picture of the demands of discipleship and what it takes to live as a faithful Christian.

We might feel that we have started our Christian life with a sprint; but should we try to keep this speed up forever, we would soon tire. For us, too, the world must retreat. We cannot encumber ourselves with things unnecessary for our journey. We tend to think that so many things about our lives are essential; but when it comes down to it, if we take the view of the athlete, much needs to be laid aside.

As we start our Christian race, we have to settle down with quiet determination to run the distance. This takes a great deal of patience and endurance. We have to be patient because we shall always be fragile people while we live this part of our pilgrimage toward and with Christ. Occasionally, things will go wrong. The convalescence from sin is a thorough but measured process. Christ is bringing God's great work in each one of us to perfection, but it will take our whole earthly lives. We need to pace ourselves and not think too much of the distance we have to cover lest it dismay us. We need to learn endurance because following Christ means living against the grain of the world, a world that offers plenty of reasons why we should give up our determination to run with Christ. It will often seem easier to slacken our pace, take other directions, or perhaps be tempted to give up all together. In these hours of weakness, what makes the greatest difference is that we are not running for ourselves or only to beat other people to the finishing line. In the Christian race, we run together with Christ and help one another as the church through those times when we need encouragement to keep up the pace.

This is one way of understanding what was going on in the hearts and minds of the Exodus people led by Moses. Having read the amazing miracles that God performed on their behalf to free Hebrews from slavery, we may feel astonished that a moment's doubt could ever have entered their hearts again. How could they have experienced all those miracles and then doubted whether God would see them through the commitment made to them? They put God to the test because they allowed themselves to question whether God was completely trustworthy. "Is the LORD among us or not?" (Exodus 17:7). Perhaps they thought that from Egypt onwards would be more of a sprint than a distance race. They wanted things to happen quickly. When faced with the first trials, their faith began to waver. They needed the distance runner's quiet determination to finish the course.

The Exodus people were still in a childish state, grumbling that God was not looking after them well enough. There would be many more instances of this lack of trust and its consequences. Moses' patience would also be tested to the limit. On this occasion, though, God answered with another miracle. The people were thirsty; therefore, they grumbled. God commanded Moses, "Take in your hand the staff with which you struck the Nile" (verse 5). The command was a reminder of previous miracles. It was, in effect, a call to Moses and to the people to remember and to trust that God would provide. God continued, "Strike the rock, and water will come out of it, so that the people may drink" (verse 6). When Moses struck the rock at Horeb, water gushed out. In spite of the grumbling and doubt, God provided for the people. God's provision of the water was more than merely a practical response to the people's thirst. It was a sign full of meaning that pointed toward trust in God, who would satisfy the most profound spiritual needs of humanity.

What we are talking about here is spiritual maturity. It is wonderful when we receive, with the simplicity of a child, God's gift to us in Christ; but children have to grow up. If God constantly provided for us without any requirement for our response of love and dedication, we would stay spiritually childish forever. Think of the delight parents feel when they watch their children taking their first steps. The steps might be a bit shaky, and there might be quite a few bumps; but when they take these first steps, they are on their way to maturity. The same God who provided for the grumbling, thirsty people of Israel, provides for us as we take our first steps of faith. We are called to go the distance by living out our faith in God as well. We can count on God to support us and to provide for us as we begin to run the long race.

What has caused you to grumble at God or to doubt God's presence with you? How did God provide for you during that time of doubt?

RECONCILED TO GOD THROUGH CHRIST
ROMANS 5:1-11

In order to pave our way into this passage from Paul, let us think again of the story Jesus told of the prodigal son (Luke 15:11-32). In the last session, we thought about the role of the elder son and his attitude to his father; and we wondered whether there is always the temptation, even for those who have received the gift of Christ, of falling back into the expectation that God owes us in some way for the faithful life we are leading.

The opening verses of what Paul has to say in Romans 5 reminds us of the younger son, his wanderings and his return. We have all been in the position of the younger son.

I do not know whether you have ever had the experience of walking down a street at night and glimpsing scenes of domestic life framed by the house windows like paintings from one of the Dutch masters. In one window, you may see a mother welcoming her children home. In another window, you may see someone sitting comfortably in front of a fire reading the paper. Perhaps you have seen that great image of domestic life: the family gathered around their table for dinner, light gleaming from the cutlery and glasses, and food arriving on steaming plates. For a person who is alone or far from home, such views through the windows may cause a pang of longing to be with them or to be at their own home with a loving family.

By his own choice, the younger son had put himself out of that warm circle of the father's home but not, as we learn from the parable, out of the circle of his father's love. God's love for us does not let us go even when we turn away from God. As the younger son sat with the pigs, his money exhausted and his hopes dashed, he could perhaps see in his mind's eye the comfortable state of those he had left behind.

The irony of abandoning God and turning to a sinful life is that such a life is slavery painted as the highest form of freedom. How slavish, conventional, and boring it then seems to obey the commandments of God. How insubstantial is the spiritual comfort of staying within God's kingdom. Sooner or later, however, the true character of this freedom is revealed. It is the freedom to be alienated from the good, the freedom to hurt and be hurt by the thorns of the world. Remember what Jesus said to his critics in John: "If you continue in my word, you are truly my disciples; and you will know the truth, and the truth will make you free.... Everyone who commits sin is a slave to sin. The slave does not have a permanent place in the household; the son has a place there forever. So if the Son makes you free, you will be free indeed" (John 8:31-32; 34-36).

These thoughts about the prodigal son give us a background to our understanding of the first verses of Romans 5:1-11. In a few deft strokes, Paul summarized all that we have learned in our readings together so far. We have been justified by faith received as a gift of grace from God through the life, death, and resurrection of Jesus Christ. Through this gift, we are peacefully reconciled to God: "We have obtained access to this grace" (verse 2). The door to the kingdom, like the door opening to the penitent younger son, stands open. As we walk through that door, we embark upon a journey that stretches out before us, a journey with God's loving commitment to us and our loving commitment to God through Christ. This journey is with God toward God in the hope of living eternally in God's restored creation.

I invite you to think again of the image of the long-distance runner. Every kilometer of the spiritual marathon, if approached with humility and with a willingness to learn from God's Holy Spirit, brings great value. Paul expressed this value clearly: "And not only that, but we also boast in our sufferings, knowing that suffering produces endurance, and endurance produces character, and character produces hope, and hope does not disappoint us, because God's love has been poured into our hearts through the Holy Spirit that has been given to us" (verses 3-5).

You can almost hear the footfalls landing—rejoice, suffer, endure, develop character, hope, love, rejoice—a circle of discipleship repeated constantly in the life and experience of the believer. However, we are always surrounded by the love of God and the guidance of the Holy Spirit who runs beside us like the most dedicated of trainers. We have been brought from a position of utter vulnerability and weakness (verse 6), no more capable than a newborn child from resisting the dangers of the world. Now through Christ, we are learning to improve our spiritual strength and stamina in the great race to which we have been called. Later in Romans, Paul says, "Do not be conformed to this world, but be transformed by the renewing of your minds, so that you may discern what is the will of God—what is good and acceptable and perfect" (12:2). As we live in this renewal, our hard work and commitment results in transformation of our inner nature. As time goes on, by God's grace, we shall have less and less that conforms us to the world; and the image of Christ, our deepest reality, will shine more clearly out of our lives.

Romans 5:9 assures us that Christ's atonement has delivered us from God's wrath; but how are we to understand the wrath of God? As human beings, we are familiar with anger. Most of us experience it as an emotion caused either by a perceived slight to our pride or through our selfish wishes being frustrated. We often direct such anger toward another person. This is obviously not the kind of anger we are to understand by the wrath of God as if God were just like us, angry for slights or selfish reasons. God's nature is love and will ever be love. God, who is just, merciful, and compassionate, desires that humans express justice, mercy, and compassion toward one another and toward all creation. God's fallen creation may well experience God's absence, alienation, and wrath rather than God's love. In Paul's thought, however, God's wrath is directed toward ungodliness and wickedness.

In everyday terms, human beings have to accept responsibility for their wrongful actions in the suffering that they cause to themselves or others. Paul says at the beginning of Romans, "For the wrath of God is revealed from heaven against all ungodliness and wickedness of those who by their wickedness suppress the truth. For what can be known about God is plain to them, because God has shown it to them" (1:18-19).

In spite of our fallen nature, in spite of our weakness, "God proves his love for us in that while we still were sinners Christ died for us. Much more surely then, now that we have been justified by his blood, will we be saved through him from the wrath of God" (5:8-9). Accepting God's gift of reconciliation through Christ moves us outside of the shadows of sin and wrath.

What does it mean to you to be reconciled to God through Christ? What connections do you see between God's gift of reconciliation and the endurance, character, and hope mentioned in Romans 5:4?

IN SPIRIT AND IN TRUTH
JOHN 4:5-42

It is difficult to know how, in human terms, we are ever to address the problem of prejudice. While in many ways we have at least become more aware of the problem, our response to it does not ever seem to go deep enough. One can try education. It is good that children receive at an early stage an approach to their fellow human beings that is not prejudiced; but one can do less as a society to counter what these same children may learn from their families and friends: the thousand different ways that prejudiced attitudes become engrained almost deeper than thought. There are so many ways that we make hurtful distinctions, that we create an "us" and a "them" without good reasons.

George Bernard Shaw in his play *Pygmalion* has one of the characters remark that whenever an Englishman opens his mouth, another Englishman despises him.[1] Here we have prejudice based on region and education. However, it could just as easily be based on skin colour, nationality, or religion.

In John 4:5-42, we encounter prejudice that existed between the Samaritans and the Jews. When a Samaritan woman approached the well, Jesus asked her for a drink. Jesus completely ignored the prejudices that would have made any other Jewish man of his time hesitate. First, no Jewish man would address a woman he did not know in a public place, still less, ask her to do him a service. Second, no Jew would have anything to do with the Samaritans. Jesus destroyed these human prejudices with his request for a drink of water. The Samaritan woman responded, "How is it that you, a Jew, ask a drink of me, a woman of Samaria?" (verse 9). Jesus was not interested in all the noise of history; he was interested in the person who was with him.

Jesus and the Samaritan woman engaged in a conversation about water, a conversation that evokes the images of the water and thirst in Exodus 17:1-7. However, Jesus spoke of living water in a spiritual sense. The woman's responses indicate that she was thinking of living water in a more literal sense. Whether she ever understood what Jesus said about water is not clear. What she did understand is that Jesus talked with her in spite of enmity and prejudice between Samaritans and Jews. He told her everything she had ever done, that is, that she had had five husbands and was currently living with a man who was not her husband. He told her that worship was not about a particular place of worship and that God is a Spirit to be worshiped in spirit and truth (verses 16-24).

Their conversation led to the woman's belief in Jesus, to her witness about her encounter with Jesus, and to the subsequent belief of many other Samaritans that Jesus was "truly the Savior of the world" (verse 42).

The story exemplifies God's answer to prejudice: to love the person who is before us as Jesus does. For Christians, love is not simply a matter of emotion or good feelings toward another. After all, how could I love someone who has caused untold suffering for others? Love is much more. We love as an act of obedience and as an act of the will. Through obeying God, we open up the possibility for God to act through us.

One of the greatest burdens that Christians have to live with is the mocking criticism of the evil things that have been done through the centuries in the name of Christ. It does not seem to help when you point out that these things were done by people with little genuine understanding that God is a God of mercy, forgiveness, and love and that these terrible aberrations are distortions and demonic parodies of faith, not faith itself. No world religion is free from this unfair criticism. I have many devout Muslim friends who lament the way their faith has been distorted almost beyond all recognition by people who have created in their own hearts a violent and vengeful god to serve their own extreme purposes.

At one stage of my ministry, I had a part-time responsibility for a maximum-security prison that was in my parish. I had three wings of the most dangerous men in the United Kingdom as my flock. I decided at an early stage that when a new man arrived, I would not look at his record until I had actually met him and that when we met I would offer him my hand. I decided to do this because I believed, and still do, that the final judgment on another human being belongs to God alone. Possibility always exists for repentance, amendment of life, and taking the step of faith in Christ. The prison authorities thought I was loopy; but, of course, being a clergyman gives you the status of a sort of professional lunatic in the eyes of the world. As I followed my plan, I did receive a good deal of abuse; but on a number of occasions, that simple gesture of offering my hand began a dialogue with the inmate. One man, tough-looking, brutalized, and brutal in his life, just burst into tears and said, "No one has wanted to shake my hand for so long I thought it would never happen again."

From a spiritual point of view, all prejudice comes from a failure to love. We do not see that all creation is in God's hands and that every human being, of whatever color, nation, or faith, even if they are your declared enemy, are all within God's providence. Even though they may be living at enmity with God, while they live on earth they are not beyond the reach of God's gift of love. Christ has opened the door to God's kingdom. We should not try to close it, dare to decide who should go in, or stand in the way of those who wish to enter.

What incidents of prejudice do you recall in your life? How did they affect you? To whom might you offer the hand of Christian friendship?

---

[1]From *Pygmalion: A Romance in Five Acts*, by Bernard Shaw (Constable and Company, 1920); page 195.

Appearance and Reality

Scriptures for Lent:
The Fourth Sunday
1 Samuel 16:1-13
Ephesians 5:8-14
John 9:1-41

One of the artistic fashions of the 17th and 18th centuries in Europe was that of the *trompe d'oeil*. Artists rivaled each other in creating pictures of things such as musical instruments or a bowl overflowing with fruit and flowers that were so amazingly realistic that the dinner guests would feel they could pick up the instrument and play it or sink their teeth into one of those beautiful apples so invitingly offered. This was no more than a bit of fun, albeit fun that required the most remarkable artistry. I suppose in our own times when we are so used to the illusions that the cinema can create, especially with computer graphics, we are harder to impress.

There are, however, darker sides to not being able to tell truth from an illusion. Sometimes people set out to deceive; and their intention is not to have a bit of fun but to profit from the other's gullibility, or worse, to do them actual harm. In the spiritual life, too, we are set the task of telling the difference between the people and choices that lead us toward God and those that are placed in our way as a temptation. We call this discernment, and it is a spiritual gift needed in a world that prides itself on its power to deceive. Deceit is a near cousin to the lie, and we know from the Gospel that we are to beware of the one who lies as an expression of his very nature (John 8:44).

Today's readings explore the contrast between truth and appearance—the latter perhaps not an overt intention to deceive, but if taken as the sole basis of judgment, something that will ultimately mislead us from Christ's path. We think about the world and values of the Spirit over against those of the flesh. In 1 Samuel 16:1-13, we hear of how the young David was chosen to be the leader of the people of Israel. In Ephesians 5:8-14, Paul instructs the church in Ephesus in practical wisdom for Christian life. Finally, in John 9:1-41, we consider many kinds of blindness that can afflict us in our physical as well as our spiritual existence.

THE LORD LOOKS ON THE HEART
1 SAMUEL 16:1-13

This story of kingship in Israel has an interesting background. God only permitted Israel to have a king in the first place as a concession to their lack of faith. If they had the King of the universe as their king, why should they require a human king to "lord it over them" in the style of other nations? We can follow this earlier in 1 Samuel 8. Samuel was old, and his sons were unsuitable to follow him; "they took bribes and perverted justice" (8:3). The people pressed Samuel to choose a king. God told Samuel, "Listen to the voice of the people in all that they say to you; for they have not rejected you, but they have rejected me from being king over them" (8:7). Samuel told the people exactly what they could expect from a human king—not an encouraging picture! The king would conscript their sons, oblige their daughters to serve in his palaces, and take the best of the crops for his own enjoyment.

Samuel anointed Saul to be the first king of the people of Israel. The tragic story of Saul is one where the high hope of having a king who could be different from the petty tyrants in nations surrounding Israel was by stages disappointed. All the dire predictions that God made through Samuel were realized. Saul ended up half-crazed by his responsibilities and his failures. He died ignominiously with his sons in battle. After his death, a war of succession continued between his house and that of David (2 Samuel 3:1).

Even after many centuries, it makes one reflect on the responsibilities we place upon our national leaders. Left to our own devices, given the situation that the prophet found himself in, we would probably be strongly moved as Samuel was to choose Jesse's first son, Eliab. We would "look on his appearance or on the height of his stature" (1 Samuel 16:7). In other words, we would look for the conventional signs of a leader; and we might make a terrible mistake. How many of us, I wonder, would reject all of these potential heroes and send instead for the boy who was looking after the sheep?

A leader is ultimately required at a moment of crisis, and we cannot rehearse a true moment of crisis. We can go through the motions and ask the "what if's?" but when the hearts begin to beat faster with apprehension and we do not know what to do, a true leader steps forward. Often in conflict, the heroes are the most unlikely people, those who might be considered weak and insignificant until they step forward in the moment when they are needed. Their action has something to do with the deepest levels of their character, the place that only God sees. God saw the character of the boy David when the people of Israel might have chosen someone who fit their own images of a leader.

As Christians, it is so easy for us to fall into this worldly way of judging human beings. Think of the way that people's voices subtly change when they are addressing someone they think is important compared to someone who is doing them a service such as repairing their cars or checking out their shopping at the grocery store. Everything about our materialist culture, unconsciously or not, proclaims, "I am different [read "better"] than you because of how I look, where I live, what I have achieved, what I possess."

In all this, in our hearts, we know where Jesus is to be found. Christians see Jesus in the servant songs of Isaiah that say "he had no form or majesty that we should look at him, / nothing in his appearance that we should desire him" (Isaiah 53:2b). In other words, the opinion of the world would pass over Jesus as if he were of no account. How many times in this life have we already met Jesus in some person to whom we have not given a moment's thought? David, the boy who watched sheep, was the last one called before Samuel. Let it not be Jesus who is the last one we call when we seek a ruler for our lives.

How do you recognize leadership skills in other people? What role does character play in your discernment of potential leaders?

CHILDREN OF LIGHT
EPHESIANS 5:8-14

In our modern cities it is quite difficult to experience complete darkness. There is always the light from office blocks, the highways, and advertising signs that continue to melt from one color to another long after anyone who could possibly be interested in them has gone to bed. One of the few times I have experienced that complete darkness was in the Sinai desert after I had crossed the Suez Canal. Without flashlights, it would have been impossible to find our way. We would not have known whether we were facing one another. While we were marveling at our helplessness in this situation, we saw a great light appear on the horizon, silently move toward us, and gradually become clear. It was a gigantic oil tanker gliding past us with every light bulb shining for all it was worth!

We are all, of course, familiar with the myriad gradations of light; it is what makes God's earth such a beautiful place. However, in the spiritual world there is no such thing as twilight. You either live in the light of God's presence or you do not. This is because, as John 3:20-21 says, "All who do evil hate the light and do not come to the light, so that their deeds may not be exposed. But those who do what is true come to the light, so that it may be clearly seen that their deeds have been done in God" (John 3:20-21).

How ridiculous it is to think that we can hide anything from God, the One who has created us, who hears every thought and sees every action, who "looks upon the heart." When we were children, we remember what it meant to have a guilty secret. Perhaps we managed to break one of our mother's favorite ornaments while she was out. We did not mean it; the ball just seemed to swerve in mid-air and sweep it off the shelf. The deed was done, and we had to decide what to do. Immediately we began to think of reasons why it could not possibly have been our fault. Perhaps we chose blind ignorance: "It was not me, I was not even at home!" Even with such a trivial thing, we experienced the circle of guilt, fearfulness, deception, and the temptation to lie— our first opportunity perhaps to take refuge in darkness.

The adult's potential for self-justification is far more developed and insidious. Often we invest so much mental and emotional energy into finding complicated reasons to excuse our actions when in fact it would be simpler, and far more honest before God, to accept our responsibility for them. People keep terrible secrets from one another. Gradually the darkness they choose to live in

steals through their whole existence. We see it so often. People who on the surface appear to be good citizens, loving parents, a force for good in the community, reveal the darkness that dwells in their hearts. We might be shocked at the time, but the wise are aware that the path to darkness is open to every human being. So, too, is the path to light.

Paul encouraged the Christians of Ephesus to "live as children of light" (Ephesians 5:8). This sounds like a pleasant occupation, a stroll over sunlit pastures. However, in spiritual terms it is demanding. Living in the light of God's holiness can often be a painful experience. The Holy Spirit gradually makes us more aware of how far, in our lives, we have fallen short of God's will. It can be hard as we begin to see our darkness.

The root of repentance is a sober understanding of how sin mars the image of Christ in us. Many people begin their Christian lives in tears of joy for the forgiveness they have received and also tears of shame and sadness about the way they have lived as strangers to God's love. The testimony of the greatest saints is that as they journey onward with God, they have had a greater awareness of God's joy and holiness as well as a greater awareness of their fragility. The tears never go away in the spiritual life; they are a sign of our humanity and neediness. Without the constant support and love of the Holy Spirit, the great adventure of faith would be over before it had properly begun. This is why, as Paul said, we should make every effort not to "grieve the Holy Spirit of God" (4:30) by returning to the sins or darkness in which we separate ourselves from God.

Think of walking in the light as a visit to Christ the healer. The first step to receiving healing is to admit that something is wrong. This, in itself, is a remarkable sign of the Holy Spirit working in our lives. When we come before Christ with that which we need to have healed, we must go through a thorough examination. Such an examination is a painful experience, but it leads to healing. God, through Christ, "heals the brokenhearted, / and binds up their wounds" (Psalm 147:3).

The works of darkness are "unfruitful" (Ephesians 5:11) because there is nothing creative about evil. All it can do is destroy. The apparent fruit of evil actions— the selfish acquisition of power over another, cruelty, hardness of heart—are things that actually destroy the person who engages in them. They think they are becoming powerful whereas in fact they are conspiring in their own ruin. Goodness and faith, by contrast, are endlessly creative even in situations where one would think all creativity would be stifled.

I am reminded of the great 20th century French composer Olivier Messiaen who was interned in a Silesian labor camp during the Second World War. Despite the

atrocious conditions during a severely cold winter, he composed, rehearsed, and performed the first performance of one of his most beautiful pieces of music. It is called, appropriately enough, the "Quartet for the End of Time." Five thousand other prisoners heard it played, and I am sure that in the depths of their suffering it said a great deal to them about the indomitable nature of a good heart.[1]

As if to show the truth of the Resurrection, God allows countless little resurrections like this to transform the darkness we cast over our daily lives on earth. He reminds us that Jesus took the worst that evil could direct at him and rose on the third day. Alleluia!

How do you understand darkness and light in your life? What does it mean to you to live as a child of light?

THE MAN BORN BLIND
JOHN 9:1-41

In John 9:1-41, we read about Jesus' meeting with a man blind from birth. We have already spent time thinking about the image of light and dark in Ephesians 5 in terms of the spiritual life. We reflected how there cannot be a twilight and that we either know God and live in God's light or we do not. In today's Gospel reading, we encounter sight and blindness associated with a miracle of Jesus.

A few words first about the miracles of Jesus. I am not of the opinion that one must look for a matter of fact explanation or a less supernatural version of Jesus' miracles. If we accept what John 1 says about Jesus—"He was in the world, and the world came into being through him; yet the world did not know him (John 1:10—it is reasonable to assume that what is natural is exactly what God chooses it to be. The miracles are rare and wonderful events, and our failure to understand them says more about our human limitations than about the power of God.

We should be aware that in John's Gospel, Jesus' miracles have a teaching, or revelatory, intent. In other words, what Jesus did reveals who he is. Jesus had ways of teaching that did not require words. There were many people who were blind in the Palestine of Jesus' time, and he did not seek to heal them all like some kind of divine health plan. The healing of the physical body points towards a spiritual reality. This account in John is one of the great signs by which Jesus reveals his divinity to those who have eyes to see.

The first question posed to Jesus by his disciples at the beginning of our reading has caused a great deal of difficulty to Christians over the years: "Rabbi, who sinned, this man or his parents, that he was born blind?" To the disciples there was obviously a strong connection between sin and the malign effects of illness or disability. To them, it

seemed like a simple cause and effect. If someone was afflicted in this way, there must be a reason. It is a mere step from this notion of sin and illness as cause and effect to that of God punishing the person through the illness. While it is reasonable to see a connection between a dissolute life and physical suffering, one could multiply forever examples of good and innocent people who suffer similar illnesses and disabilities. It cannot be their fault, nor can it be understood as a punishment for something they have done. To claim this is the case would transform our just, loving, and holy God into the worst kind of vindictive tyrant.

There is much that is mysterious about illness. Sometimes the light of Christ shines even more brightly in someone who suffers physically. Remember what God said to Paul when he prayed that his own long-term affliction be taken away: "My grace is sufficient for you, for power is made perfect in weakness" (2 Corinthians 12:9). In many ways we should understand that these things are part of the total effect of the Fall. Each of us is affected by it; but, by the grace of Christ, although the "outer nature is wasting away, our inner nature is being renewed day by day" (2 Corinthians 4:16).

I recall an incident while I was working as a hospital chaplain. I had been calling on a particular patient over quite a long period of time. He was a faithful Christian, had led a blameless and loving life but sadly was suffering from an illness that was gradually killing him. In his last days, I was often in his room even though he became less and less aware of my presence. I realized after a while, rather guiltily, that I was making time in my schedule to visit him not because he needed my help but to sit in an atmosphere of holiness that became associated with that room. I was receiving more than I was giving. On his last day on earth, even though one could see he was suffering greatly, the room felt like the center of some extraordinary power source. I had no doubt that an supremely good and powerful Presence was there. The best description I can give is that it was like sitting in full sunlight after you have spent too long in the shadows. I always refer to it as the day I met an angel.

Scientists tell us that about 80 percent of our vision is interpretation. What is presented by the optic nerve to the brain is a whirling confusion of colors, gradations of light, and dark without form or depth. What the brain then does is to interpret, to bring form out of the formless, to establish the depth between objects; and the whirling confusion becomes a flower or a human face. You get a sense of this interpretative process when your eyes begin to let you down. The brain is so used to interpreting what is out there that occasionally, if you are becoming short-sighted, it will tell you that the most remarkable things are waltzing around you. I was convinced for a long time, for instance, that a particular watering can I had was in fact a crouching cat. No matter how many times I corrected myself, my brain, when receiving this blurred image suggested "cat"—much to the amusement of my family. It does make me wonder about the reliability of our sight.

Many people report that as they journey further into the spiritual life, they are increasingly aware of the beauty of God's creation. Similarly, they see people differently; there is a spiritual discernment going on as well as the play of light beams on matter that we perceive through our eyes. Jesus' words in John 9:39, "I came into this world for judgment so that those who do not see may see, and those who do see may become blind," echo the words of God to Isaiah when he heard the call of God: "Go and say to this people: / 'Keep listening, but do not comprehend; / keep looking, but do not understand.' Make the mind of this people dull, / and stop their ears, / and shut their eyes, / so that they may not look with their eyes, / and listen with their ears, and comprehend with their minds, / and turn and be healed" (Isaiah 6:9-10).

How can people not see something (or someone) right in front of them? They do not see because even sight has something to do with the heart. We see what we want to see. If we are selfish and inward-looking, we do not see the need in others. We do not see their value; we see only what will benefit us. When we walk in the light as children of God, our senses are cleansed. We learn to see, to perceive the hand of God in our lives and in the lives of those around us.

Let us consider finally the wonder of what Jesus actually does. The man who was blind did not merely have defective sight, but he had never known what it is to see. Jesus made mud and re-created the man's eyes with his touch. If ever we needed to appreciate how difficult it is for the flesh to understand the Spirit, we need only read what happened next.

There was a kind of pantomime where some of the Pharisees tried repeatedly to fit what had happened into their understanding of God. It is like trying to force a square peg into a round hole. No matter how many times they interrogated the man or his parents, the answer was still the same. "He put mud on my eyes. Then I washed, and now I see" (John 9:15). When asked a second time, he replied, "I was blind, now I see" (verse 25). The third time he replied, "I have told you already, and you would not listen. Why do you want to hear it again?"

(verse 27). They refused to see what the man, in his simplicity, believed was as clear as daylight. This is what the touch of Jesus achieved for him.

While it was important for the man to receive healing of his physical problem, the healing went far more deeply. He was able to proclaim, "If this man were not from God, he could do nothing" (verse 33). Later, Jesus asked the man if he believed in the Son of Man, to which the man answered, "And who is he, sir? Tell me, so that I may believe in him" (verse 36). Once Jesus revealed himself to be the Son of Man, the man said, "Lord, I believe" (verse 38) and worshiped him. Jesus' work of grace and healing was complete. The man was physically healed, and his life and perceptions were changed forever.

When have your eyes been opened by God's grace in Jesus Christ? When have you been able to see God's work in your life?

---

[1]From "For Them, Time Ran Out," in *Time* (May 24, 1993); *http://www.time.com/time/ magazine/article/0,9171,978559,00.html?iid= chix-sphere.*

From Death to Life

Scriptures for Lent:
The Fifth Sunday
Ezekiel 37:1-14
Romans 8:6-11
John 11:1-45

One of the things I keep on my writing desk is a flint. This is no ordinary flint. Many thousands of years ago, sometime in the Stone Age, a human being shaped it for a particular purpose. You can see the little semicircular impact marks along the edge where one of our forebears prepared the flint to be a scraper (to remove flesh from hide) or as a convenient knife. It amazes me that it is still quite sharp after all the millennia. I keep it with me as a reminder of time—how unimaginably much time has passed already but also the way, in the "now" of God, it is only a moment ago. It also tends to put any problems I happen to have bothering me in the present into perspective.

My interest in archaeology also reinforces this inner sense of time, decay, and the passing away of generations through death. I remember watching a program where an archaeologist said that a whole vibrant city had stood where he then was; a trading crossroads, populated by tens of thousands of people.

What could you see today? Nothing. Not even a faint wall line. It was as if it had never been.

Today's readings take a long look at death as part of the order of Creation as we experience it and as the spiritual death that, if we choose, can continue from this life into the next. We begin with what appears to be the shipwreck of all human hope in Ezekiel 37:1-14. How could Israel recover from disaster? In Romans 8:6-11, we explore Paul's conception of the "flesh" and the "Spirit," where death is fully active in the former but destroyed in the latter. Finally, in John 11:1-45, we stand with the grieving disciples at the grave of Lazarus and consider again the extraordinary significance of what Jesus does.

IN GOD'S MEMORY
EZEKIEL 37:1-14

There is a place just outside the Belgian city of Ypres that the soldiers called Tyne Cot, which never fails to come to my mind whenever I read this passage from Ezekiel. Today, you can stand with your back to a memorial and gaze across green fields to the church spires and civic buildings of the modern city only five miles away. Behind you on the memorial are written in stone the names of tens of thousands of men who died between where you stand and the city walls. Their bodies were never found. Records show that they were there but that they had simply disappeared in the violence of the shelling. The mind struggles to comprehend such things. How is it that all those unique lives, those people with families and sweethearts, with their own unique histories, coming from little villages or great cities, were gone in a matter of moments? The scene in Belgium was a modern valley of dry bones like the one of which the prophet spoke where even hope seemed dead. The wind rustling over the fields seems alive with myriad whispered voices that say, "Who will remember me?"

This tragic question was one that much preoccupied the writer or writers of the psalms. The idea of death we find in many of the psalms is that when the writer passed from life all that could be looked forward to was a shadowy, insubstantial existence in the place of death, *Sheol*:

> For my soul is full of
>   troubles,
>   and my life draws near
>   to Sheol.

I am counted among those
who go down to the Pit;
   I am like those who have
no help,
   like those forsaken among
the dead,
   like the slain that lie in the
grave,
   like those whom you
remember no more,
   for they are cut off from
your hand.
                              Psalm 88:3-5

The prayer is that God will remember the psalmist. This introduces us to a much richer idea of remembering than we are used to in normal parlance. What is meant here is far more than a simple "bringing to mind" as one does when, for instance, recollecting the people you used to work with a few years ago or the children who were in your class at school. God's remembering is active and dynamic and actually keeps the person in being. That is, to be remembered by God is to have your uniqueness as a human being preserved. We continue to exist because God remembers us every day.

The implications of this are tremendous. There is our consolation when we are bereaved. Standing at a place like Tyne Cot (or, tragically, at a hundred other places where human destructiveness has been demonstrated), we can be reassured by the thought that in God's memory nothing good about those people can ever be lost. Human memories might fail, but God's memory will never fail. All of these people, from all the human generations, right back to the person who sharpened my flint, stand in God's memory.

The same holds true for the companions of death—sickness and decay. You need do no more than take a look in a mirror to be aware that the processes of aging are quietly taking place. Increasingly, at some unguarded moment while shaving, I catch the expression of my father on my own face. This is, of course, the natural way of things. Despite all the best efforts of the beauty industry, what is happening to each of us will continue to happen. While I completely understand people's desire to look the best that they can, I often feel that there is a touch of desperation about the beauty industry. Spiritually it seems to be in a kind of denial. What their advertisements imply is that the surface appearance is what is most important. Little thought is given to the beauty of the maturing person, wrinkles and all.

What does this say about our attitudes to the elderly; the disabled; or to those who, for one reason or another, cannot hope to aspire to the obsessive standards of the beauty world? They would do better to "consider the lilies of the field" that God has made beautiful (Matthew 6:28). They are perfect because they are exactly what God intends. They give glory to God just by existing, and they do not fret and fight about returning to the soil that gave them birth.

Families suffer a great deal when someone they love is affected by an illness that gradually seems to make them waste away before their very eyes. The image that they have of them in their minds when they were younger and free from illness becomes a kind of torment. This is just as true with conditions that deprive the person of their sense of self, that alienate them from their own history so that they cease to recognize those who love them most.

I recall from my hospital ministry a sprightly gentleman who was in one of the wards. He was always impeccably turned out in a suit, waistcoat, and gold watch chain. I had no idea what he had done with his life before, but privately I always called him "the Professor." Alzheimer's had deprived him of the ability to remember me from one meeting to another; but each time we met, his face lit up with a smile, and, in true British fashion, we chatted about inconsequential things and passed judgment on the weather. I was struck by the way that he offered this warm greeting to every person who came within his company. His greeting was a sign of the quality of the person who, despite the stranglehold of illness, was still very much present.

If we trust in the memory of God, we can believe that the ravages of sickness and decay only have a temporary victory. God remembers the person we love. We can be assured that our loved one is ultimately safe from all the depredations of illness and death.

If God did not remember, the prophet would have had little choice than to have been left to grieve in the valley of dry bones. He gazed with despair into the prospect of his culture's extinction. Israel as a nation was overrun many times by foreign invaders. The whole "top drawer" of society, the court, and the professional and artisan classes were forcibly removed hundreds of miles away to their invader's own country. The question was that of continuing national and cultural identity as the generations rolled by. The famous psalm on this theme says:

How could we sing the LORD's song
in a foreign land?
If I forget you, O Jerusalem,
let my right hand wither!
Let my tongue cling to the roof of my mouth,
if I do not remember you,
if I do not set Jerusalem
above my highest joy!
Psalm 137:4-6

Would their children, born in captivity in Babylon, have any care for the city of Jerusalem, which, to them, was merely a story sadly told to them by their parents and grandparents? God's answer is this vision given to Ezekiel. As the author of all life, God is capable of bringing life out of death and causing things to be that previously did not exist.

The rattling bones came together, but this was not a mere matter of revival. What is crucial here is what was written about the breath. We saw in an earlier session that the words spirit and breath in the biblical languages are the same. God did not just revive the people of Israel; God gave to them God's own Spirit, God's own breath. Without breath, the body has no life. Without the Holy Spirit, the body of the church, and every Christian who is part of it, is lifeless.

How does the promise that God remembers us comfort you as you think about times of loss or illness? How does the breath of God's Spirit and life offer you hope?

THE SPIRIT OF GOD WITHIN US
ROMANS 8:6-11

In order to understand what Paul says in this reading about the contrast between the flesh and the Spirit, it is important that we first seek to understand what he means by these terms. Language can often be a kind of tower of Babel experience in the sense that it divides rather than unites us. Occasionally, there are no perfect translation equivalents across languages. People can imagine that they are discussing one thing while those who are listening imagine something quite different.

I am reminded of a story about some of the first missionaries who visited China. They innocently set Chinese words to English hymn tunes. However, since Chinese is a tone language where the pitch of a word governs its meaning, the changing pitch of the music produced highly bizarre and even offensive meanings to the words. Even within a language amongst native speakers it can sometimes be difficult to communicate effectively. Britain has a multitude of accents and dialects for a relatively small group of islands, and it is not uncommon for someone from one part of the country to struggle to understand what someone from the same country is saying to him. I recall working as a young man in a department store where a customer asked me for what I thought were "cotton reels" whereas in fact he wanted "curtain rails." He was not pleased when I sent him off to the wrong department.

When Paul used the word flesh (sarx in Greek), he did not just mean flesh and blood existence as human beings. When he condemned the flesh as being hostile to God, he did not mean that somehow or other it is our body's fault for the trouble we get into. In Genesis 1, the body, like everything else God created, was considered "good." God has created us as beings who are body and spirit; and while we live in this life, we cannot separate them in such a way that the body is consistently bad and the spirit is consistently good.

In the past, the church has sometimes been guilty of treating the body, God's good creation, as the source of all sinfulness in human beings. This is to mistake the servant for the master. It is our sinfulness that turns something that was a good creation intended for good purposes into an agent of evil. We need only consider what we have done in our societies to the God-inspired legitimate drives of our human sexuality that, within the sacrament of marriage, become the source of joy and co-creativity with God. In our culture, the sexual drive often becomes selfish, exploitative, and ultimately life-denying.

Everything, including our physical existence, has been touched by the Fall. Paul, at the beginning of his letter to the church in Rome, identified this lawlessness in physical as well as spiritual life as a form of idolatry: "Therefore God gave them up in the lusts of their hearts to impurity, to the degrading of their bodies among themselves, because they exchanged the truth about God for a lie and worshiped and served the creature rather than the Creator, who is blessed forever! Amen. (Romans 1:24-25).

In the body we are still open to weakness, illness, mortality, and the overwhelming effects of the passions. From this we can see that "living according to the flesh" is living at enmity with God, aligned with a world that is also turned away from God.

Let us take an example from cooking. Once you have cut an

onion with a knife and perhaps touched other food with it, the taste of the onion goes right through everything. Turned away from God, sinfulness taints all our lives, even those things that we feel are the best things about us. This is a tragic situation for God's good creation, yet God took wonderful steps to correct it through death and resurrection.

The fleshly aspect of our existence, according to Paul, has to die, for how can one be said to live apart from the source of all life? It is rather like a stream flowing down from the mountains. It is clear and pure because it is constantly renewed from above. It has life and identity; although in a mysterious way, it can never be the same stream from one moment to the next. If you cut the stream off from it's source, the water remains pure only for a moment; but then gradually the light goes from it. It becomes sluggish, turbid, and at last it begins to go stagnant. This is what the Fall did to us. It cut us off from our source. The mind of the flesh thinks that stagnant water is the freshest available! Yet, in Christ, God re-started the flow of living water through our lives. We have left behind the stagnant condition of the flesh.

Paul expressed this by saying, "But you are not in the flesh; you are in the Spirit, since the Spirit of God dwells in you. . . . If Christ is in you, though the body is dead because of sin, the Spirit is life because of righteousness" (8:9-10).

Earlier in Romans, he said, "Do you not know that all of us who have been baptized into Christ Jesus were baptized into his death? Therefore we have been buried with him by baptism into death, so that, just as Christ was raised from the dead by the glory of the Father, so we too might walk in newness of life" (6:3-4).

After our baptism into Christ, what has changed about our bodily life? Are we still subject to illness and aging? Certainly. What has changed can perhaps never be stressed too strongly. When Paul said that we are a "new creation" (2 Corinthians 5:17), he was not just using impressive language; he expressed a fact of our new spiritual reality. The same idea exists in Romans 8:9-10. The life that we now live is lived by virtue of Christ's life and righteousness. While we are still open to the frailties of our human condition, they have no permanent hold on us since our true life is established eternally away from the flesh and in the life of God's Spirit that dwells within us.

What hope do you find in Paul's understanding that God's Spirit dwells within us?

POWER OVER DEATH
JOHN 11:1-45

In John 11:1-45, we focus on Jesus' friends Martha and Mary and their deep grief over the death of their brother Lazarus. The story is personal and offers solace for those times when we sit at the foot of our own Calvary and feel the loss of someone we love. It reveals God's compassion and demonstrates God's power over death, a theme that we have explored in Ezekiel 37:1-14 and Romans 8:6-11.

The picture that comes to my mind when I read this story of Lazarus and his sisters is an icon of the Eastern Church that represents the "Descent into Hades." One of the traditions of the church is that during the three days between Christ's death on the cross and the resurrection, he descended to a place like the psalmists' Sheol. These icons present dramatic pictures of Christ with his feet set upon the broken doors of hell. Scattered at his feet are usually painted the useless locks and keys that, up to the moment of Christ's passion, kept those somber and terrible doors locked. His robes shine brilliantly with the light of the Transfiguration mountain. Around him are images of the patriarchs who, while they are people who served God faithfully in their generation, had not until that moment been able to share in Christ's victory. In the foreground are our first parents, Adam and Eve. Jesus is shown grasping the hand of one or both of them, about to draw them out of this place of shadows into his glory.

What does this mean? First, one of its most profound meanings is that Christ is undoing the effects of the Fall right from the beginning. When Adam and Eve share Christ's glory, sin is cut off at the roots and the first offense disappears. As their descendants, we have our share in their humanity and in the soon to be glorified humanity of Christ.

Second, Christ has visited the deepest and most wretched places of the human condition. During times of bereavement, the words from Psalm 139 are a joyful reality:

> Where can I go from your spirit?
> Or where can I flee from your presence?
> If I ascend to heaven, you are there;
> if I make my bed in Sheol, you are there.
> Psalm 139:7-8

Again, I am reminded of the arms of the cross. The vertical dimension of the divine stretch from heaven to the deepest places of the human spirit. The horizontal dimension is that of Christ the perfect human being in his incarnation and in the activity of the Holy Spirit within the world.

Even though it seems clear that Jesus knew exactly what he was going to do when he went to meet Martha and Mary, this did not mean that he did not share profoundly in their grief. Jesus was "deeply moved" (John 11:33), and it is the only time in the Gospel that we hear that Jesus wept (verse 35).

Jesus revealed that we have a God who understands what we feel. The story demonstrates through Jesus' encounters with Martha and Mary that God-in-Christ meets us and communicates with us in the way that we can understand. Martha talked about her grief. Mary wept. Jesus engaged them and empathized with them where they were at their moment of pain. He talked with Martha. He wept with Mary.

In a previous instance of Jesus returning someone to life, the widow's son at Nain (Luke 7:11-17), it was an act of great compassion since the widow only had one son and, therefore, without him she would have had no means of support. Sadly, given the low status of women in first-century Israel, she would also be left with no name amongst the people of Israel and would have become someone who lived miserably on the edges of society. In the case of Lazarus, Jesus performed the miracle "for God's glory, so that the Son of God may be glorified through it" (John 11:4). It had a teaching intent and was a great sign of Christ's power over life and death; but it was not the greatest sign of all. That would be the Resurrection. Lazarus's resurrection, however, pointed toward the resurrection of Christ and, by extension, our own resurrection with and through him.

This is the promise that is made to each of us who have accepted Christ's life. Death will not have dominion over us. It cannot because the doors of death are broken off their hinges. Nothing good about us can be lost. We can, therefore, live as free people, unafraid of what the future may hold. The hope is offered to us through Jesus' words to Martha, "I am the resurrection and the life. Those who believe in me, even though they die, will live, and everyone who lives and believes in me will never die" (verses 25-26).

How have you experienced God's presence and power during times of loss or grief? What hope do you find in Jesus' words to Martha?

Christ's Humility

Scriptures for Lent:
The Sixth Sunday
Isaiah 50:4-9a
Philippians 2:5-11
Matthew 26:14–27:66

Our Lenten journey is approaching its goal. In previous weeks, we have tried to take a long, serious look at our spiritual life and have reflected on Christ as a teacher, healer and, more than anything else, as our Savior. We have considered the fragility of our human nature and how dependent we are on God's Holy Spirit even to take the first steps in a life of faith. Our journey, figuratively speaking, has led us around in the company of the disciples through the desert places of Judea and through the bustling towns and villages. We have seen Jesus in the uproar of crowds, in conflict with those who felt he threatened their position in society; and we have witnessed the tenderness of his care towards the sick, the disregarded, and the poor.

In the Scriptures for the sixth Sunday of Lent, we leave the countryside of Christ's ministry; and we see, like an arrow flying towards its target, Christ's determination to bring his great work on our behalf to its conclusion in Jerusalem, a conclusion involving suffering and self-sacrifice.

Rather like beams of light falling through a stained glass window, the first two readings this Sunday reveal different sides of the central narrative of the Passion. The prophet Isaiah wrote of God's suffering servant centuries before Israel even suspected that the Messiah would come. The letter to the Philippians next teaches us about the true nature of humility. Finally, we enter into a consideration of the Passion story itself. Can we hear it this Lent with fresh ears? Does God have something particular to say to us this year even though we may feel the story is familiar?

THE SUFFERING SERVANT
ISAIAH 50:4-9a

Remember right back at the beginning of Lent we were thinking about the story of Genesis with

Adam and Eve in the heavenly garden. We were turning over in our minds the profound effects of that first mistake, trusting the creature rather than the Creator, and beginning to follow the trail that led through sin and despair to mercy and forgiveness with Jesus Christ. When they had disobeyed God and eaten the forbidden fruit and were full of guilt and confusion, Adam and Eve hid in the garden. This echoes strongly the first part of our reading from Isaiah. God said, "Why was no one there when I came? / Why did no one answer when I called?" (Isaiah 50:2).

It is our own sin that exiles us from God. We hide from God in the bedlam of the world even though it is pitiful to think one could ever hide from the One who created us. The picture we have here is of God continually holding out to us the offer of love: "Is my hand shortened, that it cannot redeem? / Or have I no power to deliver?" (verse 2). Sadly, we discovered that one of the main effects of the Fall is that we had become almost impervious to what God continued to do for us. Turned away from God to a world marred by our own rebellion, our ears had ceased to hear God's voice even though, as the psalmist said, God's voice in creation is never silent (Psalm 19:1-2).

Isaiah's prophecy begins to show us how God was going to undo the wrecking effects of sin. How would God rescue the stricken creation? With claps of thunder and bolts of lightning? Would God draw all the nations of the world together in a moment of fearful judgment? While this is certainly how we expect time to come to a conclusion at the return of Christ, the beginning of the story of our salvation is so humble, so hidden, that one could easily miss it. It reminds me of the saying that the reason why we do not hear the voice of God more often is that we are not stooping low enough.

As an example of the way God speaks quietly but powerfully through the ordinary things of our lives, I am reminded of a couple who approached a colleague of mine many years ago to have their baby baptized. While the mother was eager and was obviously a faithful Christian, the father gave the impression of having been brought along against his will. He was a long-haul truck driver, quite tough looking, covered with tattoos, who evidently was putting up with all this "churchy stuff" for the sake of his wife. They started a series of preparation sessions for the baptism that father and mother attended. As the sessions went on, God touched the father's heart; and he began to hear the gospel with fresh ears. At the end of the sessions, he asked whether he, too, could be received more fully into the church. Imagine his surprise when my friend told him that the child's name Christopher in Greek meant "Christ bearer."

What we see in verses 4-9a of our reading is our introduction to the figure of God's perfect servant—the human being who takes upon himself the task of being faithful in a faithless generation and endures the consequences. The prophet developed this picture more fully in 53:2b-3 where the themes of hiddenness and freely accepted suffering remind us more powerfully of Christ and the incidents of his passion.

In Chapters 50 and 53, as well as others in the Old Testament, those faithful to God in their generation offer us an opportunity to catch a glimpse of the Christ who would come to save creation. May our prayer today be that, like the suffering servant in Isaiah, God might waken our ears morning by morning "to listen as those who are taught" (50:4).

When have you experienced the quiet voice of God? How has God supported you during times of suffering?

CHRIST-LIKE HUMILITY
PHILIPPIANS 2:5-11

Humility is not a popular concept today it seems. We live in a society that encourages us to get out there and show people what we can do. As we say in Britain, "We are not backward in coming forward!" In this context of confidence verging on pushiness, the notion of humility can become associated with those of weakness and ineffectiveness. Essentially we say, "It's all right being humble, but don't let people walk all over you!" I think we have missed the point here. Humility is, in fact, the powerhouse of the spiritual life.

Think of a sport such as wrestling or martial arts. People who engage in these sports will tell you that what is most crucial at the moment of contest is where your center of gravity is placed. If your center of gravity is too high, you can easily be knocked off balance, which explains why the contestants bend their knees and drop their bodies just before they go into the clinches. Keeping one's balance is difficult.

When I was a prison chaplain, I went along with the prison officers to learn a few simple moves in Aikido. It was for my own self-preservation so that I could escape from dangerous situations. We were a group of largish young men, and our instructor was a woman about half our weight. To demonstrate her technique she invited all of us, together, to see if we could get hold of her. To our astonishment, we simply had to give up after receiving several deft throws to the mat. Our own weight seemed to become our greatest enemy. We seemed to be incapable of keeping our feet. In spiritual terms, those who are proud are like the people who keep their center of gravity high. It takes very little to knock them off balance. What a thump they make when they hit the ground!

Humility is, in essence, a sober view of your own character. If you have that sober view of your own fragility, your center of gravity in the life of the Spirit is close to the earth from which Genesis tells us God formed the first human being. This does not mean that we go to the other extreme and have a low opinion of ourselves since we believe we are people loved by God, people for whom Christ died. What it does mean is that we are beginning to understand Christ's humility. In these terms, people who practice Christ-like humility are strong when buffeted by the high winds of the world. They know that their true strength, their center of gravity, is Christ.

Christ accepted God's will so that he could shoulder the burden of our weakness and sinfulness. He "emptied himself" (Philippians 2:7), as Paul says, setting aside any concern for his own safety or defense. For this reason, God exalted him (verse 9).

We mentioned in the previous reading how the name of a child (Christopher) became the way by which God spoke to the child's father. There is a powerful idea connected with the giving of a name in the Old Testament and the New. The patriarchs of the Old Testament received new names as a sign of being received into a new relationship with God. Abram became Abraham; his wife Sarai, Sarah (Genesis 17:15-16).

One of the most important name changes in the history of God's dealings with the Exodus people is when Jacob received the name of promise, Israel. Jacob spent the night wrestling with an angel (Genesis 32:24-32). What is fascinating is that the upshot of this unequal contest is that Jacob wanted to learn the angel's name but instead received a new one himself.

In the New Testament, we find Jesus also giving some of his disciples new names, almost nicknames that expressed some inner aspect of their characters. To Simon he gave the name Peter, which means "rock" in Greek. You will remember that Jesus did this because he saw Peter as being the rock upon which the early church would be built (Matthew 16:18). Similarly he called the argumentative brothers James and John the "Sons of Thunder" (Mark 3:17). In the early church it was common for people to be given a new name at baptism indicating a new kind of life. One way to interpret the importance of naming in the Bible and to apply to our contemporary lives is that God knows us at the deepest level of our personhood. The person who exists in the ego of every day is necessarily temporary and fugitive. The person God called into existence through Christ is eternal.

Philippians 2:9 presents the name of Jesus as a name of adoration, the name by which we know God. For this reason, the name of Jesus finds its natural place in Christian prayer. We offer our prayers through the name of Jesus. The ancient practice of the Jesus Prayer provides a way to practice our adoration. The content of this prayer is "Lord Jesus Christ, Son of God, have mercy upon me, a sinner." It is a prayer that acknowledges our true humility, and it correlates with the message of humility, obedience, selflessness, and waiting on the will of God presented in verses 5-11. If we can approach, even remotely, the example of Christ in these matters, we will have shown our love for him by example.

How do you understand humility? How is your understanding different from or similar to Christ-like humility? How might you practice Christ-like humility in your daily life?

THE PASSION
OF THE LORD JESUS
MATTHEW 26:14–27:66

Many Christian traditions structure their prayerful consideration of the passion of Christ around certain stages or stations. What I will try to do in what follows is give thoughts on three parts of the story of our Lord's passion: the Last Supper, the garden of Gethsemane, and Jesus' trial and crucifixion. Even this is a fairly tall order since one could easily write whole books about each one of these (and people have) rather than attempt to comment on them all together. I hope that by this means

I will be able to contribute to your own thoughts as you read the account again and ponder the various words and actions that accomplished our salvation.

The Last Supper: Matthew 26:17-29. In the West we have developed a craze for fast food. In the Middle East, hospitality and the sharing of food is still accorded an almost ceremonial status. As I mentioned before, I lived in Egypt for three years before I was ordained, working as a teacher of English as a foreign language. It was not long before one of my Egyptian students invited me to his family home for dinner. Being new to the country and its culture, I did not know what to expect. Nevertheless, with the optimistic ignorance of the young, I traveled to his village in the countryside outside Cairo. To my surprise, the whole village seemed to have turned out to meet me and conducted me like some local hero to the family's house.

I sat down at their table, and the dishes started to arrive in profusion. While I ate, I was observed by a fascinated audience of children who had managed to get their heads into a window of the dining room. It disturbed me after a while that none of the rest of the family were eating. I soon realized that though they were quite poor, my accepting their invitation had conferred great honor on them. I was basically eating my way through their pantry. I felt humbled and uneasy about this, but to refuse the food would have been a great disappointment to them. So, with many pretended stops and starts, declaring how full I was at every stage, I convinced them that justice had been done to their generosity. The audience of children, now swelled by their parents, noted all this with great appreciation; and judging by the beaming smiles on my hosts' faces, I assumed I had done the right thing. This was table fellowship as it is still experienced in the Middle East.

It was not so different in Jesus' day. Essentially, to accept a seat at someone's table was to say, "You are my equal." Conversely, to cast your eye over who was sitting at someone's table said a great deal about the host. This is why the Pharisees were so appalled when Jesus was content to sit with people they considered to be sinners. Recall the incident when Jesus went to dinner with the tax collector Levi (Luke 5:29-32). Jesus sat at their table because he knew they were needy people. By accepting their table fellowship he said more to them about the loving and forgiving nature of God than a thousand sermons from the Pharisees.

Table fellowship is the first thing to think about in connection with the Last Supper in Matthew 26:17-29. In the institution of the Lord's Supper, Christ offered his own fellowship to us through the breaking of the bread and the pouring of the wine (26:26-28). Today, these actions of breaking and pouring help us to recall Christ's suffering on the cross. At this last supper with the disciples, Jesus helped us by offering a way to make the Lord's Supper central to our participation in his life. He also, in a sense, has made every shared meal a sacrament if it is done in memory of him. A cup of water to a thirsty person, a simple meal to the homeless becomes, with this intention, a holy meal.

Behind the story of the Last Supper is also the great Jewish feast of Passover when the Exodus people recalled their delivery by God from slavery to Pharaoh. At Passover, the lamb was sacrificed— life for life, blood for blood. This is why Jesus said that the bread broken was his body and the wine poured was his blood. His life was offered for the life of all creation and for every human being. *How* this should be the case is beyond our capacity to understand; *that* it is the case is central to our faith. What table fellowship and Passover weave into our understanding of the Last Supper is that we are invited to God's table. The holy meal is a sign of acceptance and healing.

Gethsemane: Matthew 26:37-46. Right at the beginning of our time together, we were reminded of the paradise garden where Adam and Eve tasted of the forbidden fruit; hid from the presence of their Creator; and, tragically, were expelled. Gethsemane is the garden of decision, the garden where Jesus faced his greatest challenge. As he prayed, Jesus knew that he had been betrayed. Every moment that passed brought his enemies closer. Did he have the freedom to simply leave? Could he have gathered the disciples and melted away into the Galilean hills? I think the answer has to be yes.

If what Jesus did for us by submitting to the violence were not freely chosen, then it would be of no value. Jesus was not caught by his enemies; he waited for them to come and get him. The whole meaning of Jesus' life and ministry, his inner conviction about why he had come into the world, and what he had been sent to achieve, hung in the balance: "My Father, if it is possible, let this cup pass from me; yet not what I want but what you want" (verse 39).

The scene of Gethsemane makes me think about the nature of bravery. Sometimes in the heat of conflict, people are capable of taking risks while their blood is up. On reflection, they would ordinarily never attempt such risks. If they happen to survive, the world may call their actions brave; but in their own hearts, they may just consider themselves fortunate. However, if someone knows exactly what the risks are, knows almost inevitably that a course of action will cost them their life, and yet calmly and with determination proceed, then we see the true sign of bravery.

We cannot begin to imagine what was revealed to Jesus about what lay before him. Calmly and with determination he stayed in the garden and thus gave us the supreme example of selfless human bravery.

What can we do when the stakes are so high? We can watch and pray with Jesus. He has won the victory. The least we can do is to resist the sleep of pleasure and selfishness and spend a little wakeful time with him. What we can offer is a gift of thanks and love.

Trial and Crucifixion: Matthew 27:1-5. Every aspect of the trial and execution of Jesus reveals in stark ugliness the most perverse side of human nature. The Jewish council, the Sanhedrin, since they were subject to an occupying power, did not have the authority to pass the death sentence on anyone. The Romans generally considered local religious wrangles unimportant unless they threatened the military and economic stranglehold they had on their possessions. Hence, Jesus' accusers had to portray him as a disturber of the peace, as someone who had pretensions to being a political rival. The Romans would not execute someone for claiming to be divine. They would certainly condemn someone who might lead a popular revolt as "King of the Jews" (Matthew 27:11). Before Jesus' time they had been forced to quell at least two potential rebellions. Hence, Jesus was condemned for a political lie.

The casual barbarism of crucifixion was used extensively by the Romans. It was intended to be a punishment as well as a warning and was designed to be slow and painful. The mockery of the Roman soldiers and the scourging of Jesus were, from their point of view, part of a fairly normal day. Habits of evil and cruelty had become almost commonplace.

To the Jews, crucifixion represented a curse, as Paul said to the church in Galatia: "For it is written, 'Cursed is everyone who hangs on a tree'" (Galatians 3:13). Perhaps the most searing, bitter things to ponder about Christ's suffering on the cross are the words that are addressed to him by the people for whom he was dying: "He saved others; he cannot save himself" (verse 42). Knowing what Jesus did for us, we should say, "To save others, he will not save himself."

Which of these three scenes from the valley of Jesus' passion speaks most deeply to you? Why? What hope do you see?

The Resurrection Light

Scriptures for Easter:
Acts 10:34-43
Colossians 3:1-4
John 20:1-18
Matthew 28:1-10

Good Friday must have been a noisy day, made even more ugly and tragic by the sounds that echoed around the hill of Calvary. We think of the sounds of nails being hammered into wood, the groans of those crucified, the babble of voices from the onlookers. On Passion Sunday, we thought of the terrible things that were said to Jesus as he hung upon the cross, as he died for those who reviled and mocked him. The morning of Resurrection could not be more different.

In my imagination a great peaceful silence holds the whole earth as it awaits an event beyond the expectation of any creature. Sometimes, as I am sure you have experienced, if you are out in the countryside just before dawn, before the sound of the first bird, you catch a sense of that great stillness. The Lord has risen. Death, through attempting to swallow life, has died instead. The tomb is empty, and the promise was kept. As we have accompanied each other through Lent, it is as if we have been preparing ourselves only for this moment.

We have tried to enter more deeply into God's Word, to allow the Holy Spirit to open our eyes so that we can see and understand the great truths of our faith with a fresh appreciation. Today, for every believer, as Revelation says, "God will wipe away every tear from their eyes" (Revelation 7:17). We approach the living heart of our faith.

We begin today's readings by, in a sense, leap-frogging over the accounts of the Resurrection to hear the voice of the early church in Acts 10:34-43. Through the mouth of Peter, Christ's "rock," we hear the apostles' understanding of who Jesus is and was and the mission that lies before all believers. Particularly important for us, people separated by centuries from the Caesarea of Cornelius, is the way God showed through the gift of the Holy Spirit that the gospel is for all nations—Jew and Gentile alike. With Paul in the letter to the Colossians, we think again of the profound change that happens in the very being of every Christian when they begin to share in Christ's resurrection life. Finally, in accounts of the Resurrection in John 20:1-18 and Matthew 28:1-10, we share the wonder and joy of the evangelists.

PETER'S SERMON
TO THE GENTILES
ACTS 10:34-43

For the Jew of the first century, it is difficult to think of anyone least likely to come to mind as a possible convert to the new life of faith than a Roman centurion! Cornelius was a foreigner to them in every conceivable way. He was probably Italian by birth (perhaps even from Rome) and had spent enough time in Israel to become accustomed to, and to respect, the faith of the Jews. In their terms, he was a "God-fearer," someone sympathetic to their religion and customs but still a Gentile forever destined to stand outside the covenant.

There was also the political fact that Cornelius was a centurion in the occupying power. A centurion was an important man within the Roman army, usually someone with family connections, but also a tried and experienced soldier. His very presence in Israel was to ensure Rome's continuing domination of their country. Given what we were thinking about last Sunday in connection with table fellowship and accepting a person's hospitality, imagine what it might mean to Peter to receive an invitation from someone like Cornelius and what the rest of his people would think were he to accept. Peter was introduced to this life-changing moment through his vision of the clean and unclean animals (Acts 10:9-16). To say that Peter was perplexed by the vision and the invitation delivered by Cornelius's messengers must be an enormous understatement. Everything in Peter's upbringing and tradition would have rebelled against taking the good news to a representative of the Gentile enemy. Yet he trusted God and obeyed.

God always gives with both hands, which is beyond our expectations and often by the shattering of our limited or narrow idea of God's will for us. Certainly this was the case for Peter and Cornelius. Peter's speech in verses 34-43 is as much a revelation and consolidation of what he had understood about Christ up to that moment as it was an invitation to the Roman to become part of the Lord's family. We sense his wonder as he glimpsed God's vast merciful intent, through Christ, who is "Lord of all" (verse 36) to offer every single human being the chance of salvation.

All through the Gospels, we are aware of how the disciples understand some things immediately but then the next moment seemed to misunderstand Christ's intent. Peter himself was praised by the Lord at one moment for an insight that he had received into Jesus' true nature and then severely scolded the very next (Matthew 16:15-23).

Before the events of the cross and the Resurrection, the disciples' understanding seemed to move from light into shadow and back again. This in some way is quite comforting to us as we try to discern and understand what God is seeking to do in our lives. Even heroes of the faith like Peter struggled to grasp what was happening. However, at this moment in Acts, all the pieces are falling into place in a powerful way.

All begins from the simple yet earth-shattering statement "God shows no partiality" (Acts 10:34). The exclusive attitude of the covenant people toward the rest of humanity destroyed by Christ's death and resurrection was replaced with a glorious freedom and equality in Christ, a lived reality in the early church. Men and women, the poor and the rich, former enemies, Pharisees and sinners were united in a common life. Peter set out in the clearest possible terms the saving ministry of Christ. Jesus Christ came with a message of peace for all, a peace given by God that closes the tragic rift between Creator and creation. He went about doing good and healing people through God's power. Peter plainly described how God anointed Jesus with the Holy Spirit. The divine power was

revealed through grace and mercy to draw creation back within the circle of God's love. Against such a love even the gates of hell cannot stand.

How did Peter and the other disciples know these things? They knew them through direct experience: "We are witnesses to all that he did" (verse 39). The opening verses of the First Letter of John says of the trustworthiness of the disciples' testimony, "We declare to you what was from the beginning, what we have heard, what we have seen with our eyes, what we have looked at and touched with our hands, concerning the word of life" (1 John 1:1).

This is important for us. We do not simply believe in the Resurrection, we experience the reality of the risen Christ in our lives. Faith is a matter of experience as much as the assent of the mind. Peter described how after the Resurrection the disciples "ate and drank" with Christ (Acts 10:40-41) and received directly from him the great command to preach the good news of forgiveness of sin through Jesus Christ (verses 42-43).

As if to make the spectacular point that faith is about transforming experience, while Peter is still speaking, the Holy Spirit fell with power upon all who were listening to him (verse 44). God, once again, took the gracious initiative. May we who love God have the wisdom to follow.

What is the good news that you hear in Peter's sermon to the

Gentiles? What difference can his sermon make in your daily life?

LOOKING UP
COLOSSIANS 3:1-4

I suppose one of the reasons I enjoy walking is that there is a contemplative side to it. Like life, there are times when all you can do is keep going, plodding along a muddy track through a forest with not much to see. However, the moment comes when we turn a corner and look back in a single glance over all the distance we have traveled. That is when we say under our breath with a kind of wonder, "Have I come that far?"

When we read about the great men and women of faith, we realize that a good deal of their experiences have also been the spiritual equivalent of persevering along the muddy track. Our experience is similar. Sometimes we feel God's support and comfort close to us, and sometimes we feel as if we are required to try our own strength for a while. Even though the Christian life is impossible without grace, we are called to offer the gifts God has given to us for God's kingdom life. We are also called to offer to God, to our own lives, and to the world our determination to follow Christ, our patience in adversity, and our human courage and hope.

Through Lent we may feel that we have spent much of our time looking down, that is, mulling over the things to do with our human nature, reflecting on the way Christ came to meet us in the fragility of our humanity. Now is the time, today of all days, for us to look up. Like certain flowers that turn their faces to the sun, on this marvelous Easter Day we turn our eyes and hearts to Christ and "seek the things that are above" (Colossians 3:1). For a time we can forget the muddy tracks and the hard daily work of discipleship and reflect that in Christ we have in a real sense already arrived.

This is the mystery of the life we now live as Christians. From the outside, in the eyes of the world, we continue to hold down jobs, raise families, and pursue the things familiar to our society. However, we have become in truth a part of God's kingdom, the "treasure hidden in a field" (Matthew 13:44) and the "pearl of great value" (Matthew 13:45-46) from the moment our true life was woven into the resurrection life of Christ. Paul said this in the most powerful and dramatic way he could: "You have died, and your life is hidden with Christ in God" (Colossians 3:3).

The "things that are on earth" (verse 2) can mean many things. We could think of the beauties of God's creation that point us toward their Creator. Countless poets down the centuries have written about the perishable beauty of natural things. If we try to hold them back, they wither in one's hand. If we love the One who made them, their beauty is eternal. This is the way we look up even when our attention is upon the world around us.

However, there are other earthly things that should detain us even less. These are the preoccupations of the world in its fallen state. Rather like those sticky weeds that attach themselves to your clothing when you are out walking, the preoccupations of the world have a way of attaching themselves to even the most determined pilgrim. However, if we keep looking up, we can also see how insubstantial and feeble these things are when compared to the glory of Christ in which, even in our mortal lives, we begin to share.

Through continually repeated acts of the will, through our love for God, through the life of prayer, Christ is gradually transforming us into his image. We may not be aware fully of how this is happening in the same way that we may only occasionally be given a glimpse of how far we have come in a day's hike. God's promise of life through the risen Christ is working itself out in each of our lives. This is why Paul could say, "When Christ who is your life is revealed, then you also will be revealed with him in glory" (verse 4). The iron left continually in the fire becomes virtually indistinguishable from the fire without losing its identity. When Christ appears, we shall be the people we were created to be and glorious reflections of Christ's image.

HE IS RISEN INDEED. ALLELUIA!
JOHN 20:1-18
MATTHEW 28:1-10

One the most powerful personal memories of Easter Day that I have comes from a time I spent in the mountains above Athens in an old Greek monastery called Pentelli. I was fortunate enough to be able to spend two weeks at the monastery as their guest under the auspices of the World Council of Churches. The Easter Liturgy started in the afternoon on the eve of Easter and continued right through to about six o'clock in the morning. Imagine the scene. We had been standing praying and singing for hours on end. The small church set in a courtyard high on the hill was surrounded by a great crowd of people, perhaps as many as a thousand. Everyone was there, the oldest to the youngest children, who were playing in the courtyard while their parents walked in and out through the open church doors as the liturgy proceeded. There was a real sense of a whole community waiting expectantly to celebrate the rising of the Lord.

As the light of the rising sun began subtly to change the darkness of night into dawn, a single candle was lit from the altar; and gradually that light was shared with every person in the church, each catching the flame with his or her own candle. Once everyone's candles were alight and the great proclamation "Christ is risen!" received the joyful response of "He is risen indeed!" the people began to return to their homes. They flowed out of the monastery gates like a great river of flickering light, still holding their lit candles. Even half an hour afterwards, the attentive eye could catch the flicker of candles wending its way up a hillside lane in the distance as the worshipers neared their homes. What better image could there be of the flame of Christ springing from the tomb and going out to light the whole world?

The two accounts of the Resurrection that we have this Sunday, while different in detail, present us with important truths about our faith. The disciples—men and women—were experiencing something that quite simply went beyond their capability to understand. How, for example, does anyone give a calm, rational description of an encounter with an angel? Matthew noted the reaction of the guards: They "shook and became like dead men" (Matthew 28:4). Even though the angel sought quickly to reassure the women, they were nonetheless human and probably felt an overwhelming desire to take to their heels!

There are few human concepts that can make sense of these experiences and even fewer words to describe the indescribable. When all is said and done, we believe that Jesus rose from death because, as Christians, we experience the reality of Christ's resurrection. His is the abundant life in which we now share. Without Christ, our faith would be nothing more than a dry intellectual assent to certain moral principles. It is this life-compelling conviction that permitted the first martyrs and many Christian martyrs in our own day to proclaim the truth of Christ even when subjected to the most appalling suffering.

Think of the testimony of eyewitnesses for quite mundane events. For example, if the police are trying to get an agreed version of something that has happened, they often find it difficult indeed. How would ordinary human beings cope with the events described in the Gospel? Just because we find it difficult to describe something does not mean that it is not powerfully real and present to us. We have the same problem with love. We feel we know what it means to love someone. We can provide pages filled with things we believe accompany love. The natural scientists can even give us a biochemical slant on what is going on. However, no explanation quite exhausts the experience of loving. Something powerful and convincing happened to the disciples, something that transformed them from frightened, sad survivors of a perceived tragedy to people fearless of death with an extraordinary message to tell the world.

It is a point worth noting that in Matthew 28:1-10 and John 20:1-18, the women disciples had significant roles in the discovery and proclamation of Jesus' resurrection. In Matthew 28, Mary Magdalene and the "other Mary" went to the tomb to anoint Jesus' body (verse 1). John 20 tells us that Mary Magdalene visited the tomb and discovered that it was empty. Matthew's Gospel reports a great earthquake and a visit from an angel of the Lord who rolled back the tomb, showed the women that it was empty, and told the women to report to the other disciples that "he has been raised from the dead" (28:7).

As they left the tomb, Jesus appeared to them, greeted them, and gave them instructions for the other disciples to meet him in Galilee. In John's Gospel, Mary Magdalene reported the empty tomb to Peter and "the other disciple" (20:2). They entered the tomb, saw the linens where Jesus' body should have been, and returned home. Mary remained and wept outside the tomb. When she bent over and looked inside again, she saw two angels who asked her why she was weeping. At the moment of her great despair, Jesus appeared to her in the garden. When Jesus spoke her name, Mary recognized him. Mary gave the news to the disciples: "I have seen the Lord" (20:18). I find this appearance particularly moving. It reminds me of what we hear Jesus saying in John 10:27-28: "My sheep hear my voice. I know them, and they follow me. I give them eternal life, and they will never perish. No one will snatch them out of my hand."

I remember visiting an elderly woman in the hospital. She was a faithful Christian. During the visit, she took my hand tightly in hers and said, her eyes shining with life, "I can hear him saying my name!" This, in the end, is what our journey through Lent to Easter Day has been about: hearing at first faintly, and then gradually, with gaining strength, the Lord calling our names, calling us to fulfill the destiny we were created for, to be God's children in the world and in the world to come.

What does resurrection mean to you? How do you hear the voice of the risen Christ greeting you or calling your name?